Memories of A Man With Wanderlust

© By Bobby Potter

Composed in The United States of America

ISBN: 9780578916781

Paperback Printed and Distributed by Ingram Spark

Bobby Potter

Email: bpotter720@gmail.com

Memories of
A Man With
Wanderlust

A humorous, happy and
sad trip across the U. S.
and through the life of

Bobby Potter

*I dedicate this book to
Damon Martin Potter;
without him, my life would not
have been complete.*

FOREWORD

It has been said that if you don't know where you are going, you won't know when you get there. The intent, I suspect, is to encourage people to focus on a destination and methodically live their lives accordingly. I'm not sure whether this is possible or even wise. The world is getting smaller, things change, and new possibilities emerge that were unthought of just a decade or two ago. Doesn't it make sense to approach life with curiosity, keeping your eyes open to new possibilities? Is it even possible to commit to a single path? Like it or not, out of necessity, life is more likely about the journey, not the destination.

Bobby Potter has put this book together describing his life. It's the story of his journey. He has lived during a unique period of history, a time when, within his lifetime, the world has been truly transformed. His boyhood neighborhood is emblematic of this transformation: changing from a working-class neighborhood of modest single-family homes to a trendy, high-end, much-sought-after zip code. Think about the way people make a living now. When Bobby was born, our country had just tipped from a majority farm-based population to urban-based industry. He grew up during the 1950s when men went to work and women stayed home to work. With memories of the depression still fresh, the thought of a steady job, probably for life, was pretty attractive. Later, technology began to creep more into our lives to a point late in the century when whole new industries were regularly coming and going. Bobby's Journey occurred over these eventful years. Out of necessity and innate curiosity, he embraced new opportunities, and he learned a lot about people. Some might wonder why he took this course. Here's your chance, read the book.

Brent Poulton

CHAPTER ONE
Starting Out On The Farm

My earliest recollection of life was living on a farm in Hickman County, Tennessee. My mother, Lois Potter and father, Robert (Bob) Martin Potter were not educated people but they surely loved me and my sister and saw that we had food, shelter and clothing.

My family was very poor but as time went by, we improved financially. I owe my mother and father for what I am today: determined, strong-willed and caring. I am a success, not by money, but by family and my friends I have made through the years.

The towns we lived near were: Spot, Only and Bucksnort. *Real names, look them up.*

Mother was a small lady, about five feet tall and 100 pounds. She did not attend high school; she preferred to marry my dad at 15 years of age. All she wanted was a family to raise, which turned out to be difficult. She had two stillborn babies: one the year after I was born, and another two years later.

Mom & Dad

Dad was a high school graduate and was 21 when he married my mom. He was a small man, five feet eight inches tall and 120 pounds.

I was born in 1940 and was named Robert Eugene, but was always called Bobby. My sister Vanda was born in 1942 after a difficult delivery. Her umbilical cord was wrapped tightly around her neck. It restricted the air flow to her brain and affected her development. She can function fairly well but it limited her learning ability and speech. Mom and Dad took care of her for the rest of their lives. After they died, I took over the responsibility of making her life as comfortable as possible.

Mom took care of Vanda and I on the farm until Dad returned from his tour of duty in the Navy. Dad planted potatoes, corn and peanuts, and had two tools for farming: a plow and a mule. He would be behind the plow when the sun came up and worked until dark. Mother would make him lunch and walk it out to him at noon.

I remember Christmas in those early years. Our presents were fruit and nuts, not toys and games, but I was so happy about getting an orange and an apple. We did not get those things during the year. I didn't fret about it because I thought everybody's life was the same.

We lived in an old farmhouse built beside a steep hill that was higher than our house. We had a barn, pigpen, smokehouse and an outhouse. The house was an old board-and-batten structure that never had a coat of paint. The old wood had weathered for 75 years. The foundation consisted of stacks of rocks placed at strategic points to keep it from falling. The crawl space was open and

2

nothing prevented the wind from blowing under the house. Dad farmed about 15 acres, enough to grow our food supply. There also were a few pigs for bacon and a few chickens for eggs and Sunday dinner.

I remember those cold winter nights when the fire in the old Franklin stove would burn out. You could feel the drafts coming in through the board-and-batten siding. Mom would put so many blankets on us that we could barely move from the sheer weight. Sometimes Mom and Dad would let Vanda and I sleep with them to keep us warm. That stove was the only heat we had in that two-room house except for the cook-stove in the kitchen. Mother would fire that thing up every morning for breakfast. *Boy, that woman could cook!* The two rooms were the kitchen and the everything-else room.

Dad stored grain on the back porch to keep it dry. That attracted rats, but Dad kept them somewhat under control. He ran all of them off except one. That big rascal was setting up housekeeping. He ate a hole in the corner of the ceiling but Dad had the solution. He sat a chair in the middle of the room, placed another chair close to that chair, and rested his 22-caliber rifle on the back of that chair. He waited for what seemed like hours for the rat to stick his head through the hole. Then it happened! The rat showed his ugly head and … **BOOM!** He was a goner. I remember clapping my hands and jumping up and cheering. *My dad the hero!*

On occasion, I would walk out onto that dirt road that went by our house and look up and down and wonder … what lies around those curves and where does the road

3

go, and what is at the end of it. I found out later it is called wanderlust.

My dad bought us a baby pig to raise. I thought she was my pet but he was raising her for food. One afternoon I opened the little pigpen's gate and took her for a walk. I got a small limb that had fallen from a tree to guide her. I really thought that little twig would guide her, but this little pig had a mind of its own. She started walking down the road, *or was it up the road?* I could not control her; she just continued going down the road. I wasn't supposed to get in the road, but I was not letting my little pet get away. I don't know how far I followed her, but my dad came running around the curve after me. I was so glad to see him, even though I got a spanking.

I never wanted to admit that I could make a mistake. Proof of that was apparent one day when I asked Mom permission to go out on the front porch. She said, "Okay, but don't get close to the edge or you might fall off." Our porch was about two feet higher than the ground and did not have a railing. Mom had reason to be concerned because of the danger. This day Mom was right; I did get too close and fell off. I went back in the house with my lip bleeding and crying. She said, "I told you that you might fall off the porch." I said, "I didn't fall off — the wind blew me off."

We didn't have many visitors to the farm, so we didn't have people to talk with, or means by which to amuse ourselves. Neither did we have many toys to play with other than tin cans. I did have an old automobile tire that I rolled around to keep me occupied.

One day I was bored with just rolling the tire around and was looking for something a little more adventurous. Then I looked at the steep hill and looked at the tire and wondered what would happen if I took the tire up the hill and let it roll down. How far would it go? Here I went, rolling the tire up the hill. It was tough for a kid five years old. I made it to the top, stood it up and aligned it where it would go down the hill, past the fence, and how far is anybody's guess. I gave the tire a little push, and away it went. To my horror, as I watched the tire head toward its destination, there was a big black car parked in front of our house. Cars were almost never parked at our house. The tire hit the back bumper, ran up the trunk, onto the top, down the windshield, over the hood and continued on across the field to its final resting place. When I got to the bottom of the hill, Mom, Dad and the preacher were surveying the damage to the car. *Worst beating I ever experienced!*

At a time later on, when my little butt stopped stinging from my previous adventure, I had another wild idea. I always wondered what it would be like to ride a cow. I didn't know how to go about this little caper, but I started thinking of a plan. I headed to the barn where the cow was and opened the door and walked inside. She was standing in the middle of the small room; there was barely enough room for her to turn around. I started making my plans; there wasn't anything to stand on to reach her. I saw the rafters that ran across the entire barn. If I could get on those rafters, I could drop down on her and ride a little while. I liked that plan — what could go wrong?

I found a post and started my climb up to the rafters. I made it up okay and started hand walking (Holding onto the rafter and putting one hand in front of the other). I arrived where the cow was standing. She never seemed to notice what I was doing. There I was, hanging from the rafter, my feet about two feet above her. This will be fun, I thought. I'll ride around on her for a few minutes then hop off. It was time to go. I released my hands from the rafter and started my descent, plop, a perfect landing! The only problem: she didn't know about my plan. She panicked and ran into all four walls throwing me into the back wall. I jumped up and headed for an exit; I quickly got outside and closed the door. Wow, that was scary. I didn't get a spanking because Dad never found out about that little adventure.

Not much happened out of the ordinary on the farm, but one day a reporter from The Nashville Tennessean appeared at our house, wanting to take pictures of rural families and their lifestyle. He took some of our house, and left and came back the next day for more pictures. He also brought some clothing for Vanda and me. We dressed in the clothes that he brought, and sat at the base of our woodpile. He took some pictures of us and published one on the cover of the weekly magazine. *Our fifteen minutes of fame.*

We were still on the farm when I started my first year of school. That was when I wore my first pair of shoes. Even then, I had to take them off when I got home, so I didn't wear them out so quickly. I walked five miles each way, uphill both ways (*just kidding*). It was about two miles each way to a one-room schoolhouse. That was the biggest room I had ever seen. Of course I had not seen many at that age.

There was an outhouse about 100 yards from the school and a Civil War furnace across the road, where soldiers had made ammo for their guns. My uncle Mack (Mom's brother) was AWOL from the Navy and hiding out at our farm, so he walked with me. He was always my favorite uncle.

Dad was in the Navy for a couple of the six years we lived on the farm. Vanda started school but doctors advised against her continuing because of fear her condition would worsen.

Mom was very brave to stay on the farm those years, taking care of us without Dad.

Moving To A City

My second and third years of school were at Waverly Elementary, in the town of my dad's birth — a small town of maybe 1,000 residents. The highway leading into Waverly, Tennessee is a beautiful road lined with gorgeous elm trees. I remember bragging to the kids at school that I had just moved into a house with an indoor toilet. They informed me that all of them had indoor toilets. My mom was born in Greenbrier, Tennessee, a town actually smaller than Waverly. *The Greenbrier story will come later in this book.*

Moving To A Big City

My dad was always trying to give us a better life. When he had an opportunity for a better job offer, he was willing to relocate. Even willing to work two or three jobs. Moving seemed to become a family tradition. By my fourth grade, we had moved to Nashville, Tennessee, where I enrolled at Assumption Catholic School. Assumption was a campus with a school, church, priest residence and clubhouse for basketball and other events. Mom and Dad thought the nuns would keep me out of trouble (*It didn't work*). I was a good kid for a few years, but I did things that were not so good later in life. *More on that later*.

I fell in love that fourth grade year with the most beautiful girl in school, Teresa Dury. Wow, was she hot. She probably didn't know I existed. I heard later she became a nun. *Good for you girl.*

Moving Again

In the Potter family tradition, we relocated back to Waverly the next year. Dad made more money at his new job and bought me a bicycle. I spent my fifth and sixth grades riding my bike over the railroad tracks and to school and back.

We got our first TV when I was 10 years old. It was a big 27-inch monster. We were so intrigued by the moving pictures. We found out that we had more friends than we knew, by the number of people that stopped by to see our new entertainment device. We had three channels to choose from and we didn't have a remote to search for every time we wanted to turn it on or off. There was a button right on the front of the TV. The TV had two wires sticking out on top called "Rabbit ears" that sometimes we wrapped in tin foil to get a better picture.

Sometimes I would stop by the grocery/deli store on the way home from school. I didn't have any money but I'd just hang around and watch the construction guys buy their sandwiches and drinks. They would order bologna sandwiches on crackers and would pay the gentleman a dime. The sandwiches looked like they were an inch thick. I remember thinking that I couldn't wait to get older and earn a dime so I could buy a bologna sandwich.

Dad would take me fishing with him at Kentucky Lake; sometimes Mom would go with us. She would bring some sandwiches and cans of potted meat and her favorite, Beanee Weenees. Dad always had to bait Mom's hook because she didn't like to handle the worms.

Moving Back To A Big City

Here we go again moving back to Nashville because Dad got a new job. One lesson I learned from my dad: always keep trying to make things better for your family. We moved many times and it was always to a better house. I was eleven years old, going into a big city and not knowing what to expect. I had been enrolled at Assumption in the fourth grade, but that was different. Now I'm in school with the big kids, the seventh graders.

The summer was rough. I had no friends, and was always looking for someone with whom to hang out with. I was not good at being a loner; I needed companionship.

The neighborhood consisted of old homes that had seen better days. We moved there because it was the best my family could afford at that time. We lived on Ninth Avenue, about halfway between Monroe and Cheatham Streets. The house that we shared with another family was a yellow, two-story clapboard that had a 10-degree list. I expected it to fall any day.

I ventured out one day looking for friends and ended up on Fourth Avenue. Five blocks is a long way for a little country boy. I discovered that Morgan Park was not the best place to find friends. I approached a kid riding a bike and started talking to him. He mumbled some nasty words and hit me in the jaw. I got my butt whupped *(Southern for whipped)* that day. He didn't tell me his name but I knew he didn't want to be my friend.

More School

When school started, I finally found friends. I joined the football team and met a lot of guys. Jerry Horton was the quarterback, and boy was he good. Lawrence Hundley played the receiver position and was a great athlete. Jimmy Brannon was the fastest guy on the team. Richard (Crazy Legs) Simmons was a receiver; I was the running back, the guy that carried the ball. I was so proud. We had a good team for two years.

When basketball season arrived, some of us joined the team. Jerry and I were the guards. Two years of playing football and basketball were good for me. I remained friends with most of my teammates. *I finally belonged.*

My dad did not like me playing sports especially football. He was afraid I would get injured. I had to play without his knowledge, but he found out later when he read about me in the newspaper.

I attended church six days each week and served as an altar boy for two years. Father Richardson was my priest and a wonderful man and I looked up to him.

I did not have much self-confidence and became a follower, which is very dangerous if you follow the wrong people. It did not affect me until I reached my teenage years, as you will see in the next chapter.

CHAPTER TWO
Teen Years

I got a night job delivering meals for Central Cafe, next door to Seagraves and Kelly Drug Store. My buddies and I would get together and pool our money, call the cafe and order a six pack of beer for "Mr. Smith"; then I would deliver it to an alley and we would have a beer party. *Teen years are the stupid years.*

I got a night job later that summer operating the emergency elevator at St. Thomas Hospital. It wasn't a good experience. I didn't like seeing the victims of car wrecks, with all their broken bones and bloody bodies. But it was money and I stuck it out until school started. I had dreams of someday working in the medical field but lost interest.

Bobby ("Race Horse") Pardue was my favorite guy for double dating; he was the only one that had a car. I dated Dawahna Carney and he dated Ann Morgan. Bobby was known to have many fights and he was very jealous of Ann — so much so, that one night he saw her talking to a guy at Charlie Nickens Bar-B-Que. He walked up to him and clobbered him in the jaw, through the rolled-up window of his car.

The summer that I turned 14 years old, Richard Simmons, Bobby Pardue and I were hanging around Buena Vista Elementary School. With nothing to do, we decided to try our luck at throwing rocks at the bell on the side of the building. We hit it a couple of times, but one of the rocks went through a window. The cops were called and we went to Juvenile Hall. They didn't believe we were throwing at the bell. We got off with a warning, but I got upset for being arrested for something that was an accident. Maybe it was a dumb act but it was still an accident.

Charlie Nickens Barbecue was a Car Hop Restaurant. We would cruise through and check out the chicks and also eat the good food. They were unique in the sense that they had all black male wait staff.

Some of My Other Friends

Billy Joe (Rusty) Temple, red-headed guy with freckles and levelheaded. He always went home to take a shower at one p.m.; it didn't matter what we were doing. I spent many nights sleeping at his house. His mom treated me like I was part of the family. She always cooked breakfast for all her guests. I remember his first date with Carol Boner. He didn't stop talking about her. I knew then he was in love and would marry her. *Loved that guy. Rest in peace my pal.*

Jim Norton was a cool guy who went on to have a successful life. I live about a mile from him and Donna as I am writing this story. *You did well pal.*

Claude (Sonny) Cuturell was my 300-pound buddy. Sonny loved R&B music; we would play records for hours. *Never would let me ride shotgun.*

Carol Wild was one pretty lady. All the guys in the neighborhood wanted to date Carol. I dated her a few times, but it didn't work out. *Hope you have been well pretty lady.*

Bill Standley and Patricia Floyd were a lovely couple; they were always at CMI for dances. They married and are still together. They live near us and we have lunch together often. *Love you guys.*

Burns Boner was a good athlete who played pro baseball. I still see him occasionally at Grace Baptist Church in Springfield, Tennessee. *Burns died as I was writing this. Rest in peace my friend.*

Joe Standley was the younger brother of Bill. *Remember the Flamingo? Rest in peace my friend.*

Austin Potter was my cousin and friend. I taught his cute little girls (Tina and Lisa) to play poker. Austin also died as I was writing this. *I will miss you.*

Wesley Buttery. *Hope the cards have fallen right for you pal.*

Ronnie Morgan. *Miss seeing you at the Kalb Hollow luncheons pal.*

William (Penny) Bogle was a friend that died in a house fire at age 21.

Dawahna Carney and I dated for two years and I enjoyed those years immensely. We frequently went to a lake or river for swimming. Drive-in theaters were our favorite dates. My first love, isn't it wonderful? It devastated me when we broke up. Faye and I are friends with her and her husband, Jim Richardson.

Mr. Page was the director of Centenary Methodist Institute (CMI) on Monroe St. — a wonderful man that had the daunting task of keeping hundreds of teens in line. He did a great job. I played basketball and baseball for him.

He approached me one day and asked me to join the boxing team. I told him I was not interested in boxing, but he insisted, "Just give it a try," he said. I begrudgingly followed him downstairs to the gym. He put gloves on me and asked a guy to get in the ring with me. This guy was a little smaller than me. I was about 5' 7" and 130 pounds. We started sparring. I hit him once then he hit me five times. Then I hit him again and he hit me ten times. I told Mr. Page, "I don't think I want to box." I found out later, the little guy was Raymond Duncan, the current Lightweight Golden Glove Champion. If Mr. Page really wanted me to box for him, he should have put me in the ring with a wimp, not the best he had.

Billy Collins was a tall, skinny redheaded guy, who boxed for CMI and was a Golden Glove Champion. He later reached number two in the world ranking, behind Emile Griffith. Billy was a super nice guy and soft spoken. He and I were in downtown Nashville one night waiting for a bus and he was wearing his Golden Glove jacket. We were standing close to the curb talking when a car pulled up and stopped in front of us. There were four men in the car. The big guy on the passenger side looked at Billy and asked, "Can you back up that jacket?" Billy answered, "Yes." The big guy opened the door and extended one leg as if he was going to get out. Billy looked at me and said, in his normal low tone, "If you can take one of them, I can take the other three." The big guy wisely closed the door and they pulled off.

* * * * *

It seemed like there was always someone getting hurt or dying in our neighborhood. A young kid named Jimmy Bishop lived in one of the apartments with our family. He was a good-looking dark skinned boy that was nice to everyone. One day he was swimming in the Cumberland River and drowned. We had a slew of people coming to show their respect.

Vincent Horton, older brother of Jerry, was a couple of years older than me. I admired him very much. Many times as we were hanging at the drugstore at Ninth Avenue and Cheatham Street, he would come by to have lunch at Central Cafe. He would ask me to have lunch with him and always insisted on paying. He was a great athlete and played all sports. I especially liked watching him play basketball for CMI. William (Goober) Skinner was on that team also — what a pair! Goober went on to be a star at Hume Fogg High School.

One night Bobby Pardue and I were walking down Buchanan Street and two guys approached us and started a fight. Bobby and I didn't do well because those guys had knives. Bobby got lacerations on his arm and I received one on my side; after they saw we were bleeding, they ran away. The wounds didn't need stitches, so we walked to Ninth Avenue and Cheatham Street and saw Vincent and three other guys. We explained what happened to Bobby and me and Vincent said they would take care of them. He always wanted to take care of his little buddy. We watched as they drove off, not knowing it was the last time I would see him standing.

Devastating News

Jerry Horton came to my house and woke me early the next morning and gave me the horrible news. Vincent and the guys had gone to Cheatham Dam for a midnight swim. Vincent dove from the top of the dam and broke his neck and back, rendering him permanently paralyzed.

I'll never forget the sick feeling I felt that day. I could not understand why such an awful thing could happen to a wonderful person with so much potential. I spent many hours visiting him at St. Thomas Hospital. Later I got my driver's license and started driving and take him for long rides in my 1954 Oldsmobile convertible (*It looked like a railroad car*).

Vincent learned to make beautiful paintings by holding the brush in his teeth. Later he got enough movement out of his arm he became a great painter.

He died in his thirty-fifth year. I still believe he was one of the most caring people I've ever known. *I love you, my friend.*

Below is a sketch of me drawn by Vincent when I was 19 years old. He had just begun to draw and paint. That sketch is still hanging on my wall after 62 years. I am amazed it has survived all these years with all the moves across the country.

Bobby age 19

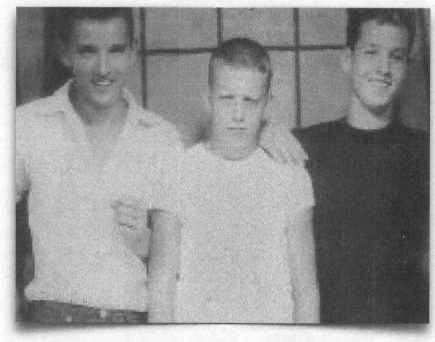

William (Goober) Skinner, Bobby Poole, Vincent Horton

CHAPTER THREE
Starting High School

After living in three different houses on Ninth Avenue in three years, Mom and dad wanted me to attend Father Ryan High School which was in West Nashville. So we moved to West Nashville. I wanted to go to North High where most of my friends were. *I lost that battle.*

My first year of high school at Father Ryan was not enjoyable, partly because I was separated from my Assumption friends. Father Ryan placed students in different levels — A, B or C. Some of my other friends went to North High. Also I was at an all-boys school. I was just beginning to notice girls were different from boys. I did well in class but when classes were over, I went to North Nashville to hang out with friends, meaning I didn't do my homework. I made good grades but because of lack of completing my homework, it pulled my average down.

I made one of the biggest mistakes of my life in my freshman year when the principal called me into the office and told me he had seen me playing a pick-up baseball game and wanted me to play for the school; I turned him down. I have regretted that decision to this day. I believe, if I had accepted his offer, I would have been too occupied to get into trouble with the law.

I missed many days of school because I stayed up late hanging around with my buddies. I made it through my

21

freshman year, but midterm of my sophomore year, I was expelled for truancy. I realized what a mistake I had made by not applying myself. I tried to enroll at North High but was turned down. I suppose my reputation preceded me. I was out of school with no friends to see during the day. Now I was really alone. Along about this time I went to church less often, attending occasionally on special events like Easter and Christmas.

Throughout my teen years, the desire to wander was with me. When I would hear people relate trips to Florida, or any place that I had not been, I would have a feeling of yearning — wanting to see what they looked like and find out what there was to do in those places.

* * * * *

Richard Townes was my best friend in my late teens and lower twenties. We were not of age to drink but we had fake IDs and we spent a lot of time together at Tip Top Drive In. Boy, did we put away some Budweisers. The bartender at that time was an ex-army guy; we called him Sarge. He told us he was investing money in Budweiser because of us. I wonder if he did; he probably would have done well.

The Lawless Years

Then the bad stuff started. The next few years I was either drinking or in jail. One night as we were riding around and drinking, one of the guys suggested we break into a service station. It scared the crap out of me, but I went along with it because I didn't want to appear chicken. Peer pressure is a powerful tool. We broke a

22

window and six of us broke into cigarette machines and stole $15. Wow what a haul, less than $3 each.

A few weeks later we were in the same car, same guys, we had a flat tire on Jefferson Street. We did not have a spare, so someone suggested we get an old worn-out tire from the service station across the street. It sounded innocent enough; nobody would mind us getting a dilapidated tire. While we were installing the tire, a cop stopped and questioned us and we told him the story. We did not consider it stealing; the tires were in a pile and looked like they were discarded. We got arrested and fingerprinted. The bad part of that situation was — I had been the only one to leave fingerprints at the service station that we had broken into a few weeks earlier. When they fingerprinted me at the station, they traced my prints to that earlier night.

I got sentenced to 11 months and 29 days in the County Workhouse. My lawyer told me, the judge didn't want to give me that much time for a small offense, but he wanted to hold something over my head. It actually made it worse for me. I knew it would be tough to do the time but I felt I could do, I have determination!

The Workhouse was the worst place I had ever been. My cell measured 8 feet by 16 feet; it had 12 bunks, a sink and a commode. We had no view of the outside world; the building consisted of three floors, eight cells on each floor. I wore chains on my ankles when I was working outside. The guards carried clubs and shotguns, and they used them both. The food was horrible, no seasoning, overcooked and tasteless — a far cry from my mother's cooking.

Someone always tested the new guys to see if they were tough. It was no different with me. After I had been in the cellblock for a couple of weeks, a guy named Bobby Bohannon decided to test me. Bobby was a tall slim guy that had a reputation for being a tough guy. We had been cordial to each other and I liked him but I guess it wasn't about feelings. It was about who was tough. I wasn't tough but I didn't like people taking advantage of me.

We kept the only valuables under our bunk (Toothpaste, toothbrush and razor). One Saturday night after the guards had left the cellblock, Bobby approached my bunk and asked to look under my mattress. I thought he wanted to borrow my toothpaste as he had done on previous occasion. Instead, he took three dollar bills, which was all of the money I had. He walked back to his bunk and said, "I'm going to keep the money because I don't think you are man enough to take it back."

I looked at him and said, "Bobby I don't want any trouble but I will not let you take my money." I got up from my bunk and closed the six feet between us and took a mighty swing at him but missed. The momentum turned me around and he grabbed me from behind, wrapped one arm around my neck and stuck two fingers up my nose and said, "We can stop this or I can rip your nose off your face." I though that was a "No brainer." So I said, "Why don't we quit." He let me go and we were friends thereafter.

Each work crew showered together, no privacy and the work was backbreaking. It was so bad that we would pray for rain. We worked on the road one day that was covered with a few inches of ice and it was nine degrees above zero.

I saw inmates intentionally injure themselves to get out of work — some would break their fingers; one man cut his hamstring, causing him to have a limp forever. Another laid his hand on a rock and asked another inmate to break his fingers with a sixteen-pound sledgehammer and he severed four fingers.

As hard as the work was, the worst part was the loneliness of staying in the cell on the weekends. I would lie on my bunk and wonder, is this what God has in mind for me? I'm not liking it.

I learned to make crafts and made a wallet using Camel cigarette wrappers. I gave it to Richard Townes as a gift in 1961. In 2007, two weeks before his death, he brought me that wallet, (In perfect condition) and said he was dying from cirrhosis of the liver and wanted me to have it back. We had a sad visit; it was difficult to say goodbye to a friend of 60 years. I hugged him and told him that I loved him and I was sorry for him. That wallet has lasted for sixty-plus years. *I miss you buddy.*

After serving three months, my parents spent a lot of money to get me out. I was released on probation. By now I was feeling picked-on and continued drinking.

I stayed out of trouble for about a year. Then one night, I was in a Seven-Eleven walking to the cashier to pay for a sandwich and got arrested for shoplifting. I had every intention of paying for the sandwich, but the police knew my record and assumed I was guilty and I was taken to jail. I was found not guilty of the shoplifting but my probation was revoked because I violated my curfew. Now I was really feeling the world was out to get me. I spent four months in the County Workhouse and my wonderful parents bailed me out again.

Many, many times the police would see me walking through the neighborhood and stop and question me. Many times they would take me to jail, although I wasn't doing anything wrong. They used a charge of vagrancy and loitering (No job, no reason for me being at that place).

Once after questioning me one cop decided to beat me. He handcuffed my hands behind my back and proceeded to pound on my face. One blow broke my nose and other blows bloodied my face so bad I had to stay home for a week. After beating me I was charged with resisting arrest and loitering. *That caused me to have a low opinion of the police.*

That continued until I left the neighborhood. One night I got drunk and rolled my car and totaled it. As the EMS guys were putting me in the ambulance, one of them said, "He will never make it to the hospital." That is when I passed out. I was checked by doctors and they found I was not injured, just drunk. That little episode scared me. I started thinking — maybe I should straighten my life up a bit.

I stayed out of the Workhouse for a year. I tried to do better but was still drinking and was arrested for DUI and sent back to the Workhouse. My parents told me they would get me out again, but I refused. I wanted to get this behind me and try to start a new life. I served five more months; that made it a year I'd spent in that hell hole. Thirty days of that year were spent in solitary confinement (The hole). In the hole I had two sleeping options — on a naked steel bunk or a concrete floor with no mattress, no blankets and no sheets. Food consisted of one piece of bread for each meal, and every third day, I got a "Full meal" — two veggies and a piece of bread.

Father Zralek, a teacher at Father Ryan, was always standing up for me. He went way beyond the call of duty for me when I was getting into trouble. He spoke to the police and judges, and anyone who could help me. *Thank you Father Zralek; I couldn't have made it without you.*

The work was tough on the chain gang: most of the work was done on the roads, working in the ditches, and cleaning drainage pipes. Some of us worked in the rock quarry, where we spent the day making little rocks out of big ones. I saw many big and strong guys pass out from heat exhaustion. The guards would drag them to the shade of a tree and leave them without medical attention. But the worst was the confinement and brutality. Beatings were common; some were unprovoked cases, like guards wanting to burn off steam.

One instance I recall, of a young black kid, about 18 years old: from my cell I could see the prisoners come in from their work detail, then one of the guards said, "Put that one in the hole." And pointed at the young black kid. The kid was not aware of the brutality of the guards and said, "For what?" The guard hit him in the head with a club. The kid started running toward his cell which was on the lower floor and he had to pass our cell to get to it. Six guards caught him and started beating him with their clubs. We had to watch this carnage through our cell bars. One guard held the kid's hand on the concrete floor while another stomped on it until his fingers were broken. When they got through beating him, and he was covered with blood, they took him to his cell downstairs.

I knew then I'd had enough. That night I sat in my cell and wrote a letter to the officials in Nashville and asked them to investigate the carnage that went on in the Workhouse. I could not send the letter out with the regular mail because outgoing mail was inspected by the guards. I was a trustee on the work gang so I could sneak the letter out. The next day, I took a chance and asked one of the truck drivers to mail the letter for me and he agreed. I was so grateful that he didn't report me. I could have spent a long time in the hole.

I really didn't think any good would come of the letter, but two officials came to the Workhouse a week later and asked for me. I met with them for a few hours and testified about all that I had seen in the months I had been in confinement. They were gracious gentlemen; most government people seemed to want to do me harm. They promised me that nobody at the Workhouse would know what I had told them and they said they would question others, to hide the fact that I started the investigation.

I went about business as usual. A week later, my truck driver buddy brought me a newspaper that contained the story of the investigation and my name listed as the person to testify. I was surprised and a little worried, as I knew the punishment the guards could inflict on me. I had about sixty days left to serve on my sentence, and as days went by, I realized I would be safe. They could not harm me because there was too much attention on the Workhouse and the guards. Major changes were made at the County Workhouse in the following months.

Vanda, Mom & Bobby (Me at 19 years of age)

CHAPTER FOUR
I Give Up, That's It, You Win

I give up, that's it, you win — that's the way I felt about the life I was living. I decided that there will be no more heavy drinking — I was going to get a permanent job and live a better life. I wanted a job and to try to find a woman with whom I could live with the rest of my life. I always wanted to be tough growing up in my neighborhood. I realized that being smart was better than being tough. I started reading and listening to smart people. I have found that if you listen to people smarter than you, someday you might be smarter also. I also learned to stop being a follower and became a leader.

* * * * *

Frankie Bogle, older brother of Penny, was a rough and tumble guy. He had a reputation of being a troublemaker and an instigator of fights. That was not true. He just didn't let people push him around. I considered him a good friend. He called one day and asked me to play golf. I said, "Are you crazy, don't tell me you're playing golf?" He said, "Yes, come and play with me." Richard Townes and I played with him that day and got hooked on golf and I could not stop playing. I still haven't stopped today. *It's your fault, Frankie. Love ya man.*

I started looking for a job but finding one wasn't easy. I had some part-time jobs, just to make enough money to get by, but I wanted a long-term job to build a future.

31

I told the employers about my past life and they didn't want to take a chance on me.

Finally, after eight months of looking, I applied at Baird and Ward, a local printing company. Human Resources told me they wanted to hire me but they have a hiring policy of hiring only high school graduates. He promised to hire me if I passed a GED exam at Vanderbilt. I took the test and passed, to my surprise! It was a tough test. The instructor congratulated me and said that some college graduates had taken the test and failed. I felt pretty good about myself.

Another Move

I started working in the bindery department and for the first time in my life, I felt I could maintain a good job. I reconnected with a friend from the old neighborhood, Joe Pyles. He didn't drink or smoke and was a good influence on me, so I left North Nashville and moved to Madison, Tennessee. I started playing golf and water skiing — clean hobbies.

I knew I would miss my old friends but I also knew that this was the right path to getting my life straight. The cops in Madison didn't know me so I felt that I would not be hassled and I wasn't.

I was water skiing at Old Hickory Lake one hot summer day and had docked my boat at the beach for a little breather. A little girl about seven years old approached me and asked if I would take her and her mommy on a boat ride. I told her that I would be glad to take them for a ride. She went to get her mommy and came back with another little girl and a beautiful blond woman. The blond woman's name was Pat. We went riding and skiing for a few hours and the girls had a great time.

We started dating and we lasted about nine months. I guess women get tired of me easily.

I had always gambled at poker, pool, and sports betting. Joe played poker at the Farmers Market in North Nashville, so I asked him to take me with him the next time he played. I made some extra money on the side at the poker table to help pay the bills. I still would have a couple of beers or a drink of whiskey on occasion, but I didn't overdo it, as had been the habit in the past. I was not an alcoholic nor was I a compulsive gambler; I did not get a thrill from winning. Gambling was a means to make money, a business.

With the lack of formal education I didn't think jobs were available to me that I could get promotions. So I gravitated toward gambling because I was good at it

I think I got my urge to play pool from my dad. He was a very good pool player and played at Sweetwater on 28th Avenue North. He was an old-school player, meaning if he could not make a shot, his opponent would not have a shot. He would hide you behind a ball in a heartbeat. His opponents called this being "Potterized." Everyone in the place knew what had happened if they heard someone yell "Potterized." I played more of an offensive game. He would frustrate me tremendously, then he had me beat

It's Getting Better

After six months in the bindery, I told management that I wanted to move up to a better job, one with a better chance of promotion. They transferred me to the press room and I liked the job but after two years, the promotions quit coming. All the pressmen were very young; it looked like they would be with the company for a long time, and I was in a hurry to make more money. I wanted to get married and raise a family. I needed to make a decent salary.

So here we go again, just like my dad, always trying to better myself — I transferred to composing; that is the department where the type is set and assembled for the presses. Now I had found something I could live with. There was the possibility of unlimited promotions. *I loved that job.*

Fishing Trip

One spring day, Joe said he wanted to go fishing at Reelfoot Lake. Billy Gerald wanted to go with us. He had just bought a new 1967 Chevelle Super Sport and he wanted to try it out. We drove the 200-mile trip only to be greeted by 40-degree weather. While we were pondering what to do, I suggested we drive south until we found warmer weather. They agreed and we drove, and drove and drove but we were still in Mississippi, so we drove still farther. Well, we ended up in Daytona Beach, Florida — we had finally found warm weather! I asked the guys if their wives would mind them going this far and both answered, "I don't know." I didn't have a wife or even a girlfriend at that time, so I didn't need permission.

We got a room on the beach at the Riviera Motel. Joe said he and his wife, Carolyn, had stayed at that motel a few times. He called Carolyn and said, "Guess where I am, I'm in Daytona Beach, Florida, at the Riviera Motel, hello, hello." I didn't think that went well. Billy called his wife and I don't think that went well either. I knew I would get the blame for this, because I was the only one of the three that wasn't married.

The next day we went deep-sea fishing, and muscled in some Red Snapper. We stayed there for a week, checking out the sights (Some of the sights were bikini clad).

On the way home, Billy tried his car out for speed. I don't remember the numbers on the speedometer, but he went way beyond the last number. A cop pulled us over and told Billy, "I'm going to give you a ticket for driving 95 MPH but I know you were going faster, but I couldn't go fast enough to get the radar on you."

We made it back okay and guess who got the blame? Billy got blamed. I never figured that one out.

I spent much time thinking about my desire to visit other cities and states. I was always asking myself, "How can I travel when I don't have enough money?" It would take thousands of dollars to do what I wanted. During the depression, hobos traveled by rail. I didn't like the sound of that. Neither can I get a job as a pilot; I'm afraid of heights and flying.

* * * * *

CHAPTER FIVE
Finding My Soulmate

My company (Baird and Ward Printing) hired new people to start computer typesetting. As I was at my work area one day, I saw one of the recently hired women pass by my department going on a break. I thought, wow that is a pretty young woman. When she went back to her department, I approached her and asked if she would go out with me and she said yes. That was the start of a long relationship. I had fallen in love. I found out her name was Scottie and she was 20 years old. She was from a small town, Fayetteville, Tennessee, and her mother was an English teacher. Her father had died when she was seven years old and had owned a shoe store in a neighboring town.

We dated for about three months and decided to get married. Wow, this twenty-seven year old country boy was finally going to take the plunge.

My luck ran out one week before our wedding day. I got laid off, after five years on the job, but we decided to continue with the wedding plans. I believe I was laid off because Scottie and I were getting married and working at the same place. No job, no money, but we had determination! We got lucky; my dad gave us $200 for a wedding gift, enough to give my bride a honeymoon.

We had sold my 1968 Firebird sports car earlier to cut expenses, so Scottie's old Chevy II clunker was the only transportation we had, so my dad graciously loaned us his new Ford Fairlane for the honeymoon trip to Florida.

We asked Father Zralek to marry us, and he eagerly accepted — what an honor to have him perform the ceremony. The wedding lasted over three hours and after all the kneeling and standing, my Best Man, Joe Pyles, later told me, "Bobby if you get married again, don't call me."

Scottie's sister Gina had a problem with the length of the service also. She almost passed out a couple of times. I guess my family and friends were not prepared for the long Catholic wedding.

We got married at Holy Name Church, and during the wedding, our friends dressed up our Chevy II with tin cans and all the "Just married stuff." We walked out of the church and got in the Ford and drove off. *Mom and dad surely looked cool driving home*.

We spent the first day in Florida on the beach. Scottie got second-degree burns over most of her body, so she laid on the bed with salve smeared over her, talk about ruining a honeymoon. She healed quickly and we had a few days of our honeymoon after all.

First Trip To Texas

When we got back to Nashville, I started looking for a job. I applied at the Nashville Tennessean. I got no promises, so I looked other places. I saw an ad for a job opening in Longview, Texas. I didn't know anything about Longview, Texas, but I gave them a call. The guy interviewed me over the phone and promised me a job if I wanted to relocate. I accepted. One of his questions was, did I know the California Job Case? I told him I had some experience with it. After I hung up; I looked at my wife and said, "What is a California Job Case?"

I had to do some investigating; I learned that a California Job Case is a drawer where type (Type is the individual letters that printers use to put ink on paper) is stored and distributed. I had used type cases before but they were Ludlow cases. The characters are arranged in order of how often they are used; each letter and number has its own little compartment. The "e" character is used most often; the "a" character is next, etc. We did not use those cases at Baird and Ward so I really had no training for them. A friend was kind enough to draw a diagram of the case and I studied it on the way to Longview. By the time we arrived, I knew it well enough to pass the test.

What Could Go Wrong?

So here we go, an old country boy and his young small-town wife, heading out into the great unknown. We knew nothing about traveling around the country, but we decided to fly by the seat of our pants and hope for the best. *What could go wrong?*

We arrived in Longview on the morning of a hot August day. I was supposed to start work at four p.m. and we still needed to find a place to stay. That wasn't easy, as we were running out of time. We saw an ad for an apartment for rent and we called and rented the place, site unseen. I asked Scottie if she would go pay them and move in. She called me at work later that night and told me a man had been shot and killed on the sidewalk in front of our apartment.

I got off work at midnight. When I arrived at our apartment, I saw blood stains still on the sidewalk. When I walked into the apartment, it felt like walking into an oven. Along with the 95-degree heat and not having air conditioning, the gas stove was on and the flames could not be turned off. We moved out the next morning and looked for another apartment. The landlord was gracious and returned the money we had paid him.

Take a note to self: *Never pay for a place to live before you check it out.*

The following day, we found a nice little apartment in a brown duplex in a great neighborhood. It had a wooden bridge across a little creek and beautiful pine trees. The owner was a wonderful lady who allowed us to pay a par-tial-rent payment. *Thank you Ma'am.*

We were so low on money that we ate bologna sand-wiches every day for a week until I got my first pay-check. We didn't even have money to turn the gas on for cooking. I remembered when I was a kid wishing I would grow up and have a dime so I could eat bologna sand-wiches. Well, now I have a dime but I don't ever want to eat another bologna sandwich.

The week went by and I got my check. We were so happy; we went to the grocery store to load up on steaks and chops and have a feast. When we paid for the food we only had $10 left. I gasped because I never knew it could be that much and we were ashamed to take anything back. As we headed home and were talking about how stupid we had been, we realized we didn't have the deposit money of $25 to turn the gas on. So, for another week we ate bologna sandwiches.

After a couple of weeks, I got a call from The Nashville Tennessean. I was offered a job at double the pay of what I was making in Longview, Texas. We appreciated the gentleman at the paper that had given me a job and the landlady that was so nice to us but we needed to accept the job offer.

CHAPTER SIX

The Road to Satisfy My Wanderlust

A fter moving back to Nashville, and going to work at The Nashville Tennessean, I joined the ITU (International Typographical Union). I learned I could go to any union printing company in the United States and find employment. *What a deal!*

At that time printers were in great demand. To move from local to local, we needed a card called "Travelers" that could be obtained from any union officer.

I talked to Scottie about traveling from city to city and she thought it was a wonderful idea. I had found my soulmate. I learned that Scottie loved traveling more than I do. Most people would be settling down, but not us; we had wanderlust!

*****

We went to visit Scottie's mother in Fayetteville, and Scottie wanted me to take my first plane ride. She knew a pilot friend of her late Dad that was willing to take us up. I was not really excited about that; as a matter of fact, I was scared out of my wits, but I let her talk me into it. We went up in one of those "Puddle jumpers" and I was sitting in the back seat; Scottie and the pilot were in the front. We were flying along and I was getting a little comfortable with flying, then things got stupid. Scottie

43

whispered something to the pilot and he reached over and turned the engine off. We went into a nose dive; I looked out the window and saw the ground coming up to meet us. They looked at me and I must have had a sick look on my face because the pilot said, "I think we should turn the engine back on." He turned the engine on and we leveled off. That was almost the shortest marriage in history; it took me a while to forgive her.

I learned later the pilot had flown in World War II and was a stunt flyer after the war. I felt a little better but I still didn't want to fly with him again.

Preparing For Our Adventure

We rented a little apartment in Joelton, Tennessee, furnished it with garage-sale furniture and saved a few bucks to get started on our adventure. We started with a partial plan: first to Texas, then to Colorado and then on to California, then who knows.

We went to see a friend, Bill Standley, who happened to be a car salesman, and told him we wanted a large car that would be good for traveling. He had the ideal car — a 1965 Buick Electra. We traded the little Chevy II and became big-car owners. Bill did well; that car served our purpose. I think it was the biggest car made at that time.

Most of our friends advised us against traveling. Some even went so far as to say we were nuts and some reminded us that we had good jobs, family and friends. Why would we leave? Our answer was, "We have a burning desire to see what is on the other side of the hill and if we don't do it now, we never will."

The traveling was good for Scottie because she was a career person and didn't like the domestic life. But that was fine with me. I liked eating out. We dined out and hired someone to clean house. It worked for both of us.

We picked up some cans of tamales for one of our first meals. She fixed them and called me to dinner. I sat at the table and saw a bowl of soup and asked, "I thought we were having tamales?" She said, "That is tamales." I inquired, "How did you fix them." She replied, "I took them out of the can, took the wrapper off and put them in the pot and stirred them." *So we had tamale soup.*

We packed our clothes in suitcases and threw them in the trunk. I cut the handle off a broom, hung it on the hooks in the back seat, that made a rod for the clothes that needed hanging. We had our entire possessions in that car and what we were wearing.

In March 1969, we headed out on our 600 mile trip to Dallas, Texas — no job, no home, not knowing what would be ahead of us. Two youngsters in love and full of determination! We shared the driving, and the passenger was in charge of the map (*The navigator*).

We were armed with a "Wage and Benefits" booklet (Printed by ITU) that contained wages, benefits, length of work week, etc. It gave us enough information to decide whether we should go to that city to work. It gave us a nut-shell overview of what to expect when we arrived.

We were like a couple of kids that just received the toy we had always wanted. I was starting something I had always wanted to do. I'm going to see what is around the next curve, and maybe see what is at the end of the road. I have my wife that is all-in for this trip and she's going to enjoy it with me.

The best word that I can use to tell how I feel driving on a road trip is: Exhilaration! We would get so excited we would wake at three or four a.m. and get on the road.

We knew one day we would have to settle down because of kids or other reasons, so we thought this was the perfect time to do something daring and enjoy doing what we will not be able to do when we are older.

Let me explain how hiring works at companies that have ITU employees:

All employees' names were posted on a board: permanent workers and substitutes (Subs). The names were lined up according to seniority; of course my name would be the last one on the board. When I applied for work, I showed my Union Card to the Union Chairman; he took my name and posted it on the sub board. If the company needed a worker for that day, I could get an office hire. If the company didn't need me, an employee could hire me to work for them. Then they took the day off or even take a week or longer off, if I would work for them. If neither needed me, I walked (I didn't get hired that day). *It works great for the company and employees alike.*

Other than time between cities, I only missed three days of work (those three days were in Houston, Texas). Those days I went to the pool hall and made a few bucks. The majority of the time I was hired permanently. If companies liked our work, we were usually hired permanently so they could get us to work every workday. Scottie never missed a day.

There are three job classifications in the Composing Department: floor men, typesetters and proofreaders. At that time, typesetting was being converted to computer typesetting. Scottie was a computer typesetter; I was a floor man.

We arrived in Dallas and found a furnished apartment on Zang Boulevard named Chateau DeVille and went to work the next day at the Dallas Morning News — no applications, no interviews, no waiting for a phone call! We just showed the Union Chairman our Union Card and went to work. We were hired permanently and worked five days a week with Monday and Tuesday off, which we used for sightseeing.

We worked at The Dallas Morning News for three months and at The Dallas Times Herald for three months.

Scottie received her Union Card while we were at The Dallas Times Herald and was able to work also. On the days we were not working, we saw as much of Texas as possible. Scottie and I had only been out of Tennessee to visit Florida, so we were amazed at the sights we saw. Scottie loved lakes, rivers and any body of water, so we stopped at all of these to take pictures. I accused her of wanting to stop at mud puddles. We would be driving on a highway and Scottie would say, "That road is interesting; let's check it out." So off we would go to check it out. That was the purpose of our travels — take our time and enjoy this wonderful land.

Texas is a great state, from the hill country in the East, to the shores of Corpus Christi and Padre Island in the South, to the Mesas of El Paso in the Northwest to the hill country in Austin. We visited every site we could in the six months we were in Dallas.

Scottie and I were compatible. We could always agree on our destination or route.

In the apartment complex where we lived, there was an apartment cat, a big yellow tomcat, fed by us and other neighbors. One night as I was coming in from work, I saw the cat sleeping on the corner of the roof, about eight feet above the ground. He was sliding so very slowly toward the edge, and I stood there for a while watching him. As he got closer to the edge, I decided to do something. That was dumb; what could I do? Well, I did the only thing I could think of at the moment. I stood under the cat, waited for him to fall; well, he fell, I caught him, I let him go; all of those things happened simultaneously. He left me bleeding all over my arms, chest and face. Why didn't I just let him fall, they always land on their feet, don't they? I told you that story because I'm not through with that cat.

CHAPTER SEVEN

Onward to Denver

T he last week of September, we left Dallas. We brought that cat (We named him Sylvester) with us, not by my wishes. (Scottie loved cats.) That cat didn't like traveling; he regurgitated a couple of times in the car, and did something much worse under the seat. I didn't think I would ever get that smell out of our car.

We didn't use credit cards, so we purchased Traveler's Checks. When we left Dallas heading to Denver, we took $600 in cash and traveler's checks and left the rest of our money in our Dallas bank. We thought $600 would be sufficient funds to last us until we received payroll checks in Denver. We also had two payroll checks that we brought from Dallas.

On the way we stopped and checked out the sights. It took us eight days to get to Denver, usually a two-day trip. We went east to El Paso, then headed north to Carlsbad Caverns. Spelunking was a favorite thing for us at that time. Then we went north to Albuquerque and Taos on the way. We spent some time in beautiful Kit Carson National Forest in northern New Mexico.

It was 103 degrees when we left Dallas and the first week in Denver it snowed 17 inches; talk about a culture shock! We were not prepared for this — no coats, no boots, but we managed after we started receiving pay.

We slugged up (Posted our name on the board) at the Rocky Mountain News. Denver was unlike Dallas. There was a housing shortage; we worked and stayed in motels, and looked for a place to live. After a week, we finally found an apartment building under construction and got one of the finished ones. There was one problem: no pets allowed. We had a solution: put Sylvester in a kennel until we left Denver. The apartment manager gave us the name of a kennel in the area. We were to move in the next day. I called the kennel and reserved a spot, so we spent one more night in the motel.

So glad to find a place, we were running out of money. The following day we headed to the kennel; we arrived about 2 p.m. and realized they had closed early. I thought it would be okay to keep Sylvester in the apartment overnight and take him to the kennel the following day. (Best laid plans of mice and men, right?) The landlady came by the apartment and saw the cat sitting in the window (Stupid cat, I told him to stay out of sight) and put an eviction notice on our door. I told her the story about the kennel but it did no good. We were back in motels, and very low on money.

We had two payroll checks from the Dallas Times Herald, but could not get them cashed. People would not cash payroll checks back in those days, especially if they were drawn from a bank in another state.

Earlier in the week I had called the bank in Dallas to send us some money, but it took a week to receive transfers. We had to open a checking account in Denver, have the money transferred from Dallas, and then we could draw it out of our account.

We got so hungry we had to resort to drastic measures. I told Scottie, "I have an idea." We went to a very nice steak house and ordered the best steak dinner on the menu. When the check came, I handed the waiter one of the payroll checks and he told me they didn't cash payroll checks. I told him that it was all we had. He called the manager and he repeated the policy of payroll checks; I told him we were hungry and had no cash. After making a few phone calls, they cashed the payroll check.

We Are Improving

We enrolled in Modern Printing Classes in Colorado Springs, about sixty miles south of Denver. We went to school during the day and worked at night. Colorado Springs is a beautiful place with a view of Pikes Peak. The Air Force Academy is a spectacular sight. The training served us well in later years.

Colorado is a beautiful state with snow on the mountains almost all year and has beautiful pine and aspen trees. The Rocky Mountains are tall, but the Smoky Mountains are more beautiful (*My opinion*).

Weather is unique in Denver. You can be enjoying 60-degree weather in downtown, then drive 20 miles to the mountains and get in a snowstorm. We enjoyed Denver but all things were not rosy.

Other than the eviction, we got our car broken into, tires slashed on our car, Scottie got her purse stolen and I got fired from my job. I received two traffic tickets —

all in 10 weeks. The job didn't matter much; I just went down the street and went to work at The Denver Post.

There are some nice thieves in Denver. The person who stole Scottie's purse put it in a mailbox to be returned to her, minus the cash.

*****

I got a ticket for an illegal U-turn. In the courtroom, the judge looked at my identification and asked, "You have Tennessee Drivers License, Texas Plates, and you are driving in Colorado, can you explain?" My answer was, "We left Tennessee in March, lived in Texas for six months, then came to Denver to go to school at ITU Training Center in Colorado Springs." He said, "Dismissed." *Nice guy, thank you, sir.*

Change of Plans

We were cold, tired and a little homesick so we decided to forgo out trip to California and go home for Christmas, and maybe take that trip at a later date. We bought Christmas presents, beautiful little bonsai trees, for our mothers. We had to turn the back seat on its side to make room for them. They had to be kept warm, so we took them into the motel when we stopped for the night. My mother's tree lived for years, but all the leaves fell off Scottie's mother's tree a week after we gave it to her. She loved that bare tree so much, she kept it until she died, thirty years later.

One of the reasons for our travels was to see if we could find a place to live that we liked better than Tennessee — if and when we wanted to leave Nashville. Although Colorado was beautiful, we crossed it off our list. *Scenery isn't everything.*

We didn't blame Denver for our misfortunes. We were young, inexperienced and did not have any plans. Not having plans is the most fun of a road trip, but there will be a few setbacks.

We hit the road to home in Tennessee for Christmas. Somewhere along the way Sylvester escaped from the car and ran into a field. We went after him, running through the field like two crazy people. (*We probably were crazy to have a cat in the car.*) After an hour of chasing him, we finally caught him and put him safely in the car.

CHAPTER EIGHT

Heading to Warmer Weather

We arrived in Nashville a week before Christmas to spend time with family and friends. We left Sylvester with my parents; they loved animals. We gave them a hundred bucks for food for the little monster. We promised to take him back when we returned from Florida. *Best money we ever spent.*

It was a good idea to spend Christmas at home. We needed time to relax and get over two months of bad times in Colorado.

Soon after Christmas, in January 1970, we left for Birmingham, Alabama. We worked at the Birmingham News for two weeks. I was offered a management job if I would stay, but Alabama was not one of the places we wanted to live. I appreciated that offer very much. We spent two days visiting friends before we left for Florida.

We were looking for warmer weather, so we headed south. We decided to stop in Tampa and watch the Gasparilla Parade. We worked at the Tampa Tribune for two weeks, and spent our time hanging at the beach and sightseeing. We checked the cost of housing, and realized it was expensive. We didn't think Tampa was a place we wanted to live.The Gasparilla Parade was great. A reenactment of Caribbean pirates.

The Real Florida

We wanted to be farther south, so we headed to Fort Lauderdale and worked for The Fort Lauderdale Sun-Sentinel. My boss invited us to dinner at his house once a week. His wife was a wonderful lady and that Cuban lady was a super cook. I love Jai alia (A sport similar to handball), and he got us free tickets weekly. I remember Las Olas Blvd., a beautiful street lined with tall palm trees leading to a fantastic beach.

This is enough to lure me to Fort Lauderdale: It has over 4,000 restaurants, 63 golf courses, 12 shopping malls, 16 museums, 132 nightclubs, 278 parkland campsites, and 100 marinas housing 45,000 resident yachts.

If that is not enough, you can find a wonderful home on the water if that is what you want.

One night after we got off work, at midnight, we drove down Las Olas Blvd. to the beach and were strolling on the beach and enjoying the beautiful moon-lit night. There were no lights, just the moon, but we could see well enough to walk. We walked by a couple on a beach towel. Scottie kept walking but I stopped and watched. She came back to see what intrigued me. It was a couple doing something that is usually reserved for the bedroom. She grabbed me by my arm and pulled me away not allowing me to look any longer. *Bummer.*

As usual we spent our time sightseeing and enjoying Florida. We went on a trip to beautiful Key West. It's such a wonderful drive, across all the bridges and beautiful water. We loved our many trips to the Everglades also. We primarily drove the back roads, for better scenery and less traffic. *I love Fort Lauderdale.*

We stayed in Fort Lauderdale for three months. I wanted to live there the rest of my life but the cost of living was very high. We earned enough money to meet basic expenses but we wanted to save more. Besides, we still had wanderlust. We kept Florida on our list of places where we might want to live at a later date.

On To Daytona Beach

After Fort Lauderdale, we decided to work in Daytona Beach. We got an apartment across the street from the beach and awoke every morning and walked across the street and basked in the sun.

I loved working at the Daytona Beach News. People were so nice and the owner even came to the Composing Room to work with us. *Talk about hands-on.*

We had a cool neighbor — a young man in his 30s, who sat on the front porch in the swing at our building and kept his motorcycle parked beside him. One day I stopped and said hello and asked him, "Why do you sit on the porch so much." He replied, "I pick up chicks." I asked, "Why don't you go to the beach and pick up chicks?" He said he believes his way was better. He continued, "I just sit here swinging and sooner or later a girl will pass by and she will ask me to take her for a ride on my motorcycle. If I like her I will take her up on her offer." *That cat was cool.*

Back to Nashville

We arrived in Nashville in April. After a couple weeks' work, I wanted to go to Cincinnati, Ohio, but Scottie wanted to stay in Nashville. I went alone and worked for two weeks. I didn't want to stay any longer; that city was colder than a well digger's butt in Idaho.

One good thing came out of that trip. I asked a fellow traveler which city was his favorite to work and live, and he said, "Knoxville, Tennessee." I was surprised; I had never thought of living in Knoxville.

I called my wife and told her I was stopping in Knoxville and working at The Knoxville News Sentinel for a few days. I was at my job one day, and a guy came over and introduced himself as Jack Oody, a very pleasant person. He also invited me out for a beer after work. I enjoyed talking to him and we have been friends since that day in November 1970. Jack is one of the finest people I have known in my lifetime. Thank you Jack, for being my friend.

Finding A Home

After working for five days, I called Scottie and asked her to pack, because we were moving to Knoxville. I drove to Nashville and we packed the car and moved to Knoxville. We arrived in town and she went to work and met some wonderful people also. *We loved the Smoky Mountains.*

58

I want to tell you a secret: when you are married, the man gets blamed for everything. Here is a good example:

One day Scottie and I were riding in Knoxville. I was driving; she was reading the paper and as we rode by the treatment plant, she smacked me in my head with the rolled-up paper, I asked, "What the heck did I do?" She said, "You know, you let one." We can't win guys, but we love them.

I had been on the road since 1969, and wanted to settle down, at least for a little while and Scottie agreed. We liked Knoxville so much we bought a cozy little 900 square-foot home in Colonial Village in South Knoxville, with a big screened-in back porch. It was a beautiful place with a large picture window looking out at a huge crabapple tree in the front yard and several white and pink dogwood trees. Our living/dining room measured 25' by 16'. We also had an eat-in kitchen. *We were home.*

The home was beautifully kept. We made a den in our third bedroom, an 8' by 10' space. We had room for a couch, chair and a TV. It was perfect for our needs.

We did our usual sightseeing and exploring East Tennessee. We bought a redwood chalet in Hidden Mountain outside Pigeon Forge to enjoy on our days when we were not working. It was a cozy little A-frame with two bedrooms and wood fireplace. A wonderful deck on two sides; our back yard was at the end of a 100' drop-off directly under our back deck. I remember a few times we heard footsteps on the deck only to find it was animals just passing by. Thankfully none were bears.

We were enjoying the life of being settled down for a change. Jack and I started playing golf and bowling and I started playing poker with Tom Bromley: three of my favorite sports.

Jack and I would go to Ruby's bar and have a couple of beers after work. The paper hired a new sportswriter — a young man who just got out of school, and he was very quiet. One night he came into the bar and ordered a beer and sat down in the booth with us. I had a pint of mountain moonshine that someone had given me. I didn't want it so I gave it to him; he had a couple of small glasses and got up out of his seat and started telling stories in a loud voice. He then stood on the bar and started talking like a Southern politician running for public office. I had never seen such a change in personality as I saw that night. I drove him home in my car and Jack followed to bring me back.

I saw him the next day sitting at his desk with his head down. I said, "Hello" and he said, "Don't talk to me; I slept in the bathtub last night and I have a headache." My response was "Welcome to the Smoky Mountains, buddy." I don't think he ever came back to that bar.

Scottie called me at Ruby's bar one night and said, "Someone is trying to break into the house." I said, "I'll be right there." I rushed to my car and raced the 10 minutes home. As I walked to the house I noticed the front door was open, oh no, someone has broken in I thought. I walked in and Scottie was sitting on the living-room sofa. She had a knife in each hand and looking tense.

Looking at the back door I noticed it was also open. I asked her, "Are you okay?" She said, "Yes." I said, "Did anyone break in?" She said, "No." I was puzzled and asked, "Why are you sitting on the couch with both doors open?" She answered, "If someone does break in I want to be sure I have a way out." *I guess that makes sense.*

I searched the house and the outside and found no sign of anyone being near the house.

*****

Tom Bromley was an awesome bowler; his average was 207 at that time. We were in a morning league; he was on one team, and I was on another. He also was a very good golfer. We had some great matches.

The city bowling tournament was coming up. I talked to the guys on my team about entering. Three of them told me they had made plans to join other teams. Where was their loyalty? The other member told me he would join me and would recruit his brother, and I got two more guys. In the process of picking a name for our team, someone suggested "Dummies" because nobody wanted us. *We became "The Dummies."*

We were one of the first teams to bowl on the opening day of the tournament; lo and behold, we set the high score that day. The next day I had mixed feelings about the sports headlines in the paper, **DUMMIES LEAD CITY BOWLING TOURNAMENT**. I was proud of leading the tournament but ashamed we didn't find a better name.

The other teams bowled for four days and could not top our score; we won the tournament and strutted around for weeks.

The only gambling I did was a poker game at our house once a week. Scottie complained about it and told me she didn't think I was making any money. I asked her, "Let me play six months and you keep track of my winnings and losses and we will check the total." After six months, the average winning total was $24.90 an hour. *Pretty good money for 1972.*

* * * * *

Scottie and I were driving on Gay Street one day and she saw an attractive woman walking on the sidewalk. As we passed her Scottie said, "She had pretty hair didn't she?" I answered "I don't know I didn't get that high." She swung the newspaper again, she missed that time because I saw it coming and ducked. *No sense-of-humor.*

* * * * *

I found that there are great people in this country no matter where they live. Scottie and I went to Cincinnati to bowl in the Honke Bowling Tournament. The second day we ran out of cash and only had Traveler's Checks. We stopped at a diner to eat breakfast and asked if they would take the checks. The waitress said, "No we only take cash." We thanked her and headed for the door. She stopped us and said, "If you want breakfast I will pay for it." I was amazed that she would offer, she knew we were from out of town and still paid for our breakfast.

We went back the next day and paid our debt and she told us that she didn't think she would see us again but couldn't let us go hungry. We ate there every day for the next two weeks. *Thank you lady for being who you are.*

All Good Things Must End

In 1974, The Knoxville News Sentinel had plans of locking the union out, so we decided to leave town and move back to Nashville. We really hated to leave; we loved our jobs and Knoxville and especially our friends. We knew we would survive, we had determination!

We sold our house to a nice young couple that was just starting out in married life. Part of the closing agreement was, I would paint the house trim. The house was a beautiful little place with dark brown cedar shingles with white trim. *We loved the cedar siding.*

I hired a young man to do the painting, and paid him up-front because he said he needed the money. I watched him work for about thirty minutes and it looked like he was doing a good job. I left for work around three p.m. and got back about one a.m. and went to sleep. I awoke about eight hours later to a phone call; the guy buying our house was chewing me out about the lousy paint job. I knew nothing of what he was talking about but I went outside and checked it out. I saw white paint splattered on my cedar shakes on all four sides of the house. That so-called painter had made a mess.

I went looking for the painter. He was not at home and his mother said she didn't know where he was. After looking for him for three days, I decided to paint it myself. It took me three days to get the job done.

We closed the deal and Scottie and I moved out three weeks later and moved back to Nashville.

We came back to Knoxville for a visit a month later and decided to ride by our old house. As we approached the house we got a shock. They had covered the beautiful cedar shingles with vinyl siding. (*I hate vinyl siding.*) Scottie lost it; she walked to the door and knocked. The young lady opened the door, then Scottie asked her why they put vinyl siding on the house after her husband had complained so loudly about paint being on it and he had worked three days to repair it. The lady said she didn't like it either, but a high pressure salesman had talked her husband into replacing the cedar with vinyl. Scottie was feeling better after venting, so we left.

CHAPTER NINE
Back Home In Nashville

W e rented an apartment on Due West Avenue in Madison, Tennessee, and signed a six-month lease, while we contemplated our next move. Joe asked me to help him with booking football; I agreed. After a few weeks, Scottie left me. She could not handle the gambling. I never lost at gambling. I might have had a slow time but I never lost for a long period of time, and never had a losing month. I believed that this marriage was forever, like Mom and Dad but it was getting rocky.

I had lost my soulmate, but I did what I have always done and put on my big-boy britches and stayed strong. I decided I would not get a job. I played pool, poker and booked football to make a living. I had determination!

Joe and I played poker almost every day — how long we played was determined by the competition. If the game had good players, we stayed until we felt we had made the maximum amount possible. If the players were not-so-good, we stayed until they ran out of money.

Other days we would go water-skiing, weather permitting. I loved being out in the fresh air on the water. We usually went to the dam at Old Hickory Lake.

I spent about a year in Nashville. I did not enjoy life without my wife, so after eight months of separation,

I called her and offered to quit gambling. She agreed to give it another try.

Going South Again

We thought a vacation would get us going again, so we headed to Florida. On the way we decided to stop and work in Macon, Georgia for a short time. It was a good place to work; we enjoyed it very much and the people were very nice. *Love southerners.*

We got our first paycheck and I looked to see how much I earned for 15 hours. My check was $1,500. I thought, wow, they're paying me $100 an hour (A lot of money in 1975) — it must be a typo. Later, we found they had inserted 150 hours instead of 15 hours. We decided not to say anything about the check until the following day.

We had the nicest foreman but he was difficult to understand because he stuttered, especially when he would get excited. The next day we walked into the newspaper like normal. The foreman was waiting for us and asked for my paycheck. I told him, "I deposited it in the bank this morning." He said a few words that I could not understand and headed to the office — I assumed to stop payment of the check. When he came back, I gave him the check and smiled.

The Union Secretary had a little fun with him also, before I arrived. He overheard the foreman talking to payroll, and told them, "If you are talking about Bobby Potter, he came to me early this morning and said he and Scottie were leaving town." *There went that stuttering.*

Each day on the way to work, Scottie and I usually ate at H&H Restaurant on Forsyth Street — great Soul Food and the friendliest people around. The owners were Inez Hill and Louise Hudson (Hence the name H&H). They were friends with the Allman Brothers Band members, especially Gregg.

We worked about two months and then something wonderful happened — we got pregnant. After eight years of marriage, we finally got pregnant. I was beside myself. I think I grew up a little that day. I had a big responsibility coming my way. From now on our traveling will be more of the vacation variety.

We decided that Florida would not be the best way to go at this point. We should not be thinking about having fun; we needed to do what was best for the baby. Houston, Texas was really booming at that time and housing was reasonable, so in December of 1975, we set our sights on Houston.

Although I still had wanderlust, now that I was going to have a child, I wanted to settle down and give him or her a stable life. I think travel is wonderful but moving too often is not good for children. Every time we moved when I was a child, I had to make new friends.

CHAPTER TEN
Time to Face Responsibility

W e got a job at The Houston Chronicle, and started making our plans. We bought a house north of Houston. After about seven months, I went to work at Fidelity Printing. I worked there for five weeks, and then something amazing happened to me that gave me direction for the rest of my life; I got fired. Yes, that was great; let me explain.

One of My Best Decisions

I applied for a job at Bowne Printing Company (also called Bowne of Houston). The largest financial printing company in the world, with offices in most major cities, and it also was a nonunion company. Normally not wanting to work for nonunion companies, but I decided to take a chance. If I didn't like it, I could go back to The Houston Chronicle and work. Bowne had been a company since 1775.

A financial printer is a specialty printer that prints legal forms for public companies. Some of the forms are: Annual Reports, 10-Ks, mergers and buyouts. Every company on the Stock Market is a public company; anyone can buy into that company and join in on the profits or losses. I learned about the Stock Market and started investing. That became the source of most of my retirement funds.

The foreman Richard Kohlhauff gave me a test and hired me on the spot. I went to work the next day. My immediate boss was Les Morrill, pronounced "Moral." I always told him he was named correctly because he had less morals than anyone I knew. We are friends to this day. *Love you Les.*

I worked there for over 20 years, then transferred to Bowne of Nashville for five more years. Working at Bowne was like working with family. We were often having parties and get-togethers. Christmas parties were great. We had a company picnic each summer.

Two weeks after going to work at Bowne, on May 31, 1976, my wife gave birth to a beautiful boy. My birthday was June 2. Scottie's birthday was June 3. If he had been born five hours later, we would have had June 1, 2 and 3. We had joked about what we would do if our boy was red-headed. There was red hair in the Scott family, Scottie's uncle. My answer was we don't pay the bill and they will keep him. Well, he did have red hair and blue eyes; we decided to keep him anyway and named him Damon Martin Potter. (Martin was my dad's middle name.)

Damon was conceived while we were on the road traveling. We have our birthdays close together and Damon spelled backward is Nomad! *I thought that was odd.*

He was born at Jefferson Davis Hospital (sometimes called "The Baby Factory") in Houston, Texas. 10,000 babies born there yearly. I figured they knew what they were doing, so that's where I wanted my baby to be born.

I took that little baby in my arms and told him, "I will bust my butt to take care of you and give you the best life I can possibly give."

He was a wonderful baby, seldom cried. Scottie was so worried about the lack of crying that she talked to the doctor about his quietness. The doctor told us to be thankful and not worry.

Mom and Dad drove to Houston to see Damon when he was about six weeks old. Dad did not like to travel but nothing could keep him away for that little boy. They stayed a couple of weeks with us and I showed them the sights of Houston.

Another Devastating Blow

I believe Scottie had a problem with me playing pool on my days off which caused problems with our marriage. We seemed to have a happy marriage when we were on the road, then when we settled down we had problems. Six months after Damon was born, Scottie and I separated, She was awarded custody, with me seeing him on alternate weekends. We agreed on the separation, but we did not divorce. I was not in a rush to divorce because I didn't think I would ever marry again.

I kept the house and Scottie moved to a new place. A couple of friends moved in with me, Paul (Yogi) Wilsey and O.G. Brown. I loved them and both are now deceased. I always told O.G. the reason for his name was his mother took one look at him at birth and said, "Oh Gee." O.G. had recently moved to Houston from St. Louis and needed a place to stay until he got settled. It worked out for me because they were good company. O.G. had new-born twin sons, Bobby and David. They stayed with me for a few months until his wife arrived.

I had some lady friends over the years, but they never lasted long. I had an on-and-off-again relationship with Ruth and raised her daughter, Donna. Donna was a sweet girl and was six years old when I met her mother. I raised her for 10 years, until she married Todd Hilton and moved to Brookhaven, Mississippi. Ruth was not with me this entire time. I vowed never to marry again and I would just play the field, so to speak. I still needed companionship. I had some girlfriends but if things got serious I moved on. The women were like me, wanting companionship but not marriage.

Donna would never ask me to give her money, she asked, "What can I do to earn some money?" I loved that about her. She was wonderful at helping me with Damon.

I was careful to not allow myself to get close to any woman. I didn't want any more hurt.

When Damon was about five months old, I took him to Tennessee to see his grandparents. I did something I normally wouldn't do; although I am terrified of planes I booked a flight. It was a hot August day in Houston when we boarded the plane. Everything seemed fine and we took off and didn't get out of sight of the airport. The captain announced we were returning to Houston, for minor repairs. We landed and they confined us to our seats on the plane for 45 minutes in the heat without air conditioning. They never told us what they were repairing.

We finally took off and headed to Nashville. I was terrified that the so-called repair would not remain repaired. The flight crew loved Damon and passed him around among each other. I saw very little of him until we landed in Nashville.

Dad met me at the gate and greeted me with these words, "I heard about the fire." I said, "What fire are you talking about?" He led me to the window and showed me the black marks on the plane that the fire had made, from the engine to the tail. They let me fly on a plane that had been on fire, with my six-month old child? *I didn't fly again for 17 years.*

Low Point of My Life

After I returned to Houston I temporally went into a deep dark world. I was feeling sorry for myself and started drinking heavily because I had lost my family; which was the glue that kept my life together. My life's desire was to have a family, a good job and a nice house. I had all of that. But now my family was gone.

One night I was especially feeling low and came home from drinking all night and pulled into my driveway. I sat in my car for a few minutes thinking about my life. I was so down on myself I decided to end my pain. I reached under my seat and pulled out a 38-calibre revolver and cocked the hammer and started slowly raising it to my temple … **BOOM!** The gun discharged and the tremendous blast of the shot was so intense it jarred me back to my senses. I looked at my car door and saw a bullet hole in the window molding. I realized the gun fired before I raised it to my head. I sat there in shock for what seem like an eternity before I could muster enough strength to go into the house

I arose the next morning trembling and thinking about what I had tried to do the night before. I realized I had not lost my family. I had only lost half of my family, I still had my son and he needed me. I started to think of Damon rather than of myself.

* * * * *

When Damon was about four years old, he said something that made me think he might be a mathematical genius. We were on the road one day (Of course we were on the road) and he said he had to use the bathroom. "Okay," I said, "We will stop at soon." He said, "Dad you don't understand — I have to do number three," I questioned him, "What is number three?" Ten he answered, "When you do number one and number two at the same time." *Smart kid.*

Scottie and I stayed separated until 1980; then she filed for divorce and I did not contest it. Scottie and I remain friends to this day. She is also friends with my present wife, Faye. She even recommended Faye marry me. *Go figure.*

Scottie and I could not be husband and wife, but that did not mean I should not like her. I have treated her as a friend since our divorce.

There is too much hate in this world to dislike someone because we can't live with them. And on that note, I believe, if you love someone, you should tell them you

74

love them. After they die, it is too late. My Father never told me he loved me and I wish I had that memory.

* * * * *

I needed to make some extra money, so I started gambling again. I lived by myself, so why not? I played pool, poker and booked football bets.

I loved playing pool. I was very good and I had a knack of knowing who I could beat; like poker, it is more about knowledge than ability or luck. I started playing pool when I was 14 years old. I learned how to shoot pool, **not how to play.** There is a difference. I remember the day I learned **how to play.**

It was during my separation from Scottie, in 1974. I was playing at Wall's Drive In on Thompson Lane in Nashville. I was hanging out with a friend, David Laine, one of the best players in Tennessee. I was playing the guy that owned the pool hall, John Wall and I wasn't doing well. He was cleaning my plow, and I remarked to David, "I don't understand why I can't beat this guy." He said, "Because you don't know how to play." (David didn't beat around the bush.) I was 31 years old, and had been playing since I was 14. I thought I knew how to play, so I said to him, "Well why don't you show me?" He said, "Okay, follow me." We went into the back room where there was a private pool table. He showed me some things I never knew you could do on a pool table.

He spent about a week working with me and told me he thought I could beat most of the people in the area.

I tested it out by challenging John Wall that night, and beat the socks off him.

*****

Coors Beer Company sponsored a pool tournament in Houston, and it started with each participating bar and pool hall having a tournament to establish their best player. 7,000 players entered and vied for the championship. There were regional tournaments that brought the total down to 250 players and I won my regional playoff. The lucky players would go to the Astrohall (A circular building next to the Astrodome). I was one of those lucky 250 players and headed to the big event.

The games were to be eight ball and nine ball. The winner would be determined by the best four out of seven. I won my first match of nine ball, 4-2. I lost my next match of eight ball, 4-3, which eliminated me. But I was proud of finishing in the top 125 Best Players in Texas.

I stayed and watched the rest of the matches and saw Bobby Brown win it all. I saw Bobby a few days later and challenged him to a best-of-seven match. He beat me four and two. It was a fun match.

In all the excitement, I didn't remember which door I had entered, and since the building was round, it was hard to tell the difference in each door. So I picked one and went into the parking lot and walked around the building for two hours. Finally enough people had left so I could find my car.

*****

I knew the risks of swimming and wanted Damon to be safe so I gave him swimming lessons at age 18 months. It was easy for him like everything else in his life. That eased my mind and allowed him to respect water but not fear it.

We made many trips to Galveston Beach. He loved the water and playing on the beach. We had picnic lunches on the hood of my car many times. He was sitting in the water one day when he was about three years old and was stung by a Jelly Fish. He screamed so loud I thought a shark had bitten him. Being a redhead he also had problems with his light skin and had to be covered with sunscreen when he was outside.

Scottie and I spend time on week-ends with Damon as a family. One particular day when Damon was about five years old, Scottie needed to visit her former home to check about mail delivered to her prior home by mistake. I drove her to the home and let her out in the driveway and Damon and I sat in the car and waited. The lady answered the door. Scottie being the talker that she is, started talking so we waited 20 minutes. Upon her return to the car, Damon asked her, "Mom what did she say?" Scottie answered, "I don't know, she doesn't speak English." Damon looked at me with a puzzled look. Even a five year-old knew that didn't sound right.

Damon came to visit every other weekend and other times whenever possible. He gave me great joy. I took him to see his grandparents once or twice a year: my parents and Scottie's mother. Those hours of driving on the road with my son were precious. We had long talks about school and life in general.

I craved Krystal hamburgers and pork bar-b-cue while in Houston because they were not available there. When we visited Nashville, I would always get both as soon as possible. On one trip with Damon, when he was about five years old, we stopped and he ate his first Krystal, and said, "Dad can we take a million of these back to Texas with us?"

When Damon was about seven years old, he, Scottie and I were walking into a restaurant and saw a Federated Electronic store. The neon sign wasn't working properly and alternate letters were burned out of the word Federated (F d r t d). Damon casually looked up and said, "They must not have paid their vowel bill." *Clever kid.*

An evening out at Papasito's Seafood Restaurant, five of us were having dinner, two adults and three children. We had a couple of drinks and ordered our meals. I had steamed clams. As I was eating I bit on something metallic. I pulled it out of my mouth and examined it. It was a wire about an inch long and bent into a hook shape. I had no idea what it was and neither did anyone else at the table. I said, "I'm afraid to eat my clams because there could be more wires in them." Damon said, "Don't worry Dad, they only catch them once."

After calling the manager, she checked with the kitchen staff and deduced that it was a wire broken off the sieve which is used to dip the clams out of the steaming grease. The manager informed us our entire meal was on the house.

Along about his fourth grade, Damon was having trouble in school. He was hyperactive and disruptive in class. I believed he needed discipline, so Scottie agreed to allow him to live with me for a year. I visited the principal at school to talk about his situation and told him he had my permission to spank Damon if necessary. The situation never came up. I worked with him in conjunction with the school for the year and he was fine.

I was called to the school one instance because he was disrupting the class. I took him home and we sat on the couch and I explained what he had done wrong. I told him I loved him and I was going to spank him for being rowdy. After a few little pats on his bottom with a wooden ruler, I told him again I loved him and told him to go to his room and come and see me when he feels like talking. Fifteen minutes later he came to me and told me he loved me and he would behave in class in the future.

Big Change is Coming

Two years later, he was having a problem again. I offered to allow him to live with me again. She said she had a better idea — "We three will live together and see if we could help him," After careful thinking about it I agreed. A platonic relationship, separate bedrooms and all, we rented a home in The Woodlands, with option to buy. We never acted on that option.

We stocked the pantry and kitchen with fruits and veggies to encourage Damon to eat healthily.

Scottie's mother taught Damon to play the piano. He liked to play but never cared enough to make a career of playing. Whenever he saw a piano that was not being used, he would sit down and start playing.

He was a problem solver. One day Scottie needed to move a large sofa from the garage into the house. The only door it would fit through was in the front. It was too bulky and heavy to pickup. Damon went to his room and returned with a basketball. He raised one end of the couch and positioned the ball under it. He pushed the couch, rolling the ball with it, repositioning when needed. He moved that couch out of the garage, over the driveway, up the walkway and through the front door and into the living room. He was eleven years old.

We tried the arrangement for two years and it worked well; it served its purpose, but Scottie wanted to move to her own place. I told her I would agree if Damon would live with me. We decided to end our joint arrangement. I bought a house in The Woodlands, with the idea of Damon staying close to his mother and he came to live with me. I was happy I had my son living with me.

New Age In Printing

Around 1984, Bowne decided to change to computer typesetting. I really liked computers, so I learned the job quickly. There was one catch — I did not know how to type. The company started classes for the people who didn't have previous typing experience, and required at least 45-words-per-minute. I was not very fast, maybe 35-words-per-minute. I kept practicing, but did not improve. The pressure was mounting; if I didn't reach the minimum words per minute, I would lose my job.

Then the weirdest thing happened — I got scratched in my eye by my girlfriend's kitten; that almost gave me permanent damage. I wore an eye patch for a few weeks, not knowing the extent of my eye damage. I did no typing during that period. I got the patch removed and learned I had no permanent damage. When I started typing again, I felt really relaxed, and asked for a test and I reached 50 words per minute!

* * * * *

It is strange bad things happen to me to cause great things to follow. The bad things must be my decisions and the good things must be God's decisions. It also has given me confidence to handle diversity.

I was fascinated with computers. We used an imbedded code system and I liked trying to see what I could make that machine create by the codes I entered. I read the manuals over and over until I had every code memorized. I would even come in on my days off to practice. I would be the only one in the building.

I was booking bets to make a little extra money. It was small time stuff, but one day the Vice Squad walked into my office and arrested me for gambling. I got out on bail and called my boss, Doyle Womack, who was also my friend and mentor. I asked if I was fired, and he said, "No, but the big boss (Tony Pepe) wants to talk to you." That made me nervous. When I got back to work, I went into his office, fully expecting to get a good chewing out. Well, he asked me to take a management job. Wow, how did that happen? I go from possibly being fired to getting promoted to Shift Manager. I got a raise and didn't need a side job anymore. So I quit gambling, paid a fine and concentrated on my job. I started working 12 hours a day, for my extra money. (Talk about falling into a garbage dump and coming out smelling like lavender.)

While I was considering the management job, I thought of my son. I had rather he see me as a manager rather than as a gambler. I wanted him to have the best chance in life possible. Hopefully my cleaner lifestyle would rub off on him. Also, I insisted on changing my hours from 4 p.m. starting time to 8 p.m. starting time, so I could see Damon off to school and have dinner with him at night. For the next 20 years, I worked with my son's future in mind.

We experimented with using two managers for three shifts. Don Campbell worked for 12 hours and I worked the other 12 hours. It worked great for work flow but it was tough on Don and I because of the long hours of stress. That lasted about six months. Later I was promoted to Department Manager

* * * * *

Six Flags Over Texas was having their annual hiring expo that summer so I drove Damon to apply for one of the openings. When the lady found out he was only 15 years old, she said, "We don't usually hire anyone under 16." He told her, "I can make you a very good employee, I work smarter not harder." She hired him.

Damon played tennis in high school so we sent him to Tennis Camp several summers in San Marcos, Texas for a week. One time I drove him there on Sunday afternoon. I took my little black and tan Dachshund with me to keep me company on the way back. She was a great traveling companion. She just laid in the passenger seat and slept. She was black and the upholstery was black and she almost disappeared.

After leaving Damon at the Camp and heading home, the traffic had increased greatly and it had gotten dark. I was driving in the left lane about 75 MPH and saw a man dressed in jeans and white tee shirt, standing on the center line of Interstate 75. He was lunging at the cars as they approached him. He looked at me as I came close and was in a position of a football tackler and acted like he was going to tackle my car. His actions were of someone having a death wish. Of course that terrified me and I moved to my left as far as possible. He lunged at my car; I gripped the steering wheel and my thought was, don't let the impact wreck me. I didn't feel anything so I continued on. As I looked back and saw other drivers swerving, that made me think he was safe. *A great relief.*

What I think is interesting about this story is this: I saw a movie once about a woman running over a pedestrian and leaving him for dead. As she drove along, she started seeing the man everywhere. She looked in the rearview mirror and saw the image of his bloody face; she panicked and ran off the road and crashed.

I started thinking about that movie scene as I was driving on the dark road, thinking about the poor man in the jeans and tee shirt and hoping he didn't get hit by anyone. I had this eerie feeling like I was in "The Twilight Zone." I was afraid to look in the rearview mirror.

I had forgotten about my dog being in the seat beside me I had my arm laying on the armrest and she touched her cold nose to my hand. I screamed at the top of my lungs and jerked my hand, swerved and almost ran off the road (surprised I didn't give my dog a heart attack by my screaming). I gained my composure and got the car under control and headed home. The next day I checked the news stories to see if anyone was hit on I-75. There was no news of anyone being hurt in that area. *You can't make this stuff up.*

* * * * *

When Damon was 18 years old, he got a job at The Woodlands Country Club as a waiter. After working there for three years, he met the head of Bill Heard Chevrolet. He asked Damon to come to work for him as a salesman. Damon took him up on the offer. That was Damon's start in car sales, which he stayed in for years.

Another Sad Time In Life

In 1994, I got a call informing me my Dad had died from prostate cancer, which he had suffered with for 15 years. I knew it would happen but it was a terrible shock. I went to the funeral home as soon as I arrived in Waverly. The shock of seeing him lying in the casket was too much; I broke down and cried. I had not cried since I was a little kid. I made up my mind then that I would never let my friends and family see me in a casket. I will be

84

cremated! Less stress less expensive and you can have a memorial at any time you wish.

I took two weeks off from work and spent a lot of time thinking about moving back to Tennessee. I made up my mind I would come back to spend time with my mother before she died.

I had been in Houston for 21 years. Damon was now 21 years old and an adult. He was working at Bill Heard Chevrolet and could support himself. I had stayed in Houston for two reasons: first, I had a son to raise, and second, I had a good job. I had accomplished what I set out to do — raise my son and get myself financially fit to retire. Not only could I retire, I changed my family tree.

I was only fifty-five years old, not really old enough to hang it up so I asked my company to transfer me to Nashville but I was turned down. I told them, "I will retire consider this my two weeks notice."

I'd had enough of the traffic, crowds and heat. It was so hot in the summer you could walk outside and be soaking wet almost immediately. Houston was good to me; I made a good living for 21 years, and I raised a wonderful son. I asked him to come with me to Tennessee but he felt like he should stay with his mother. I was okay with that because I thought Scottie would move back to her home state soon. That has not happened as of this writing.

In December 1997, as I was getting everything ready to leave, Joe Morrow, a manager from Atlanta, Georgia which was one of our offices, called me. He said he had heard I was retiring and asked me to reconsider and come to work for him at Bowne of Atlanta. I informed him I wanted to work in Nashville because it was my hometown. He said there were no openings in Nashville, but he had a job waiting for me in Atlanta.

After I thought about it for a couple of days, I decided Atlanta was better than Houston, only 250 miles from my mother compared to 800 miles. I could drive to see her on weekends, so I called him and accepted the job.

Three days later I got a call from Joe again; he said he had talked to the people in Nashville and they were going to create a job for me at Bowne of Nashville — the best news I could possibly have heard! I moved back and I had the honor and pleasure of spending five wonderful years with the woman I admired.

CHAPTER ELEVEN

Going Home

I transferred to Bowne of Nashville so it was the same work, just a smaller office. I loved my job in Nashville — super people to work with and a great boss to work for, Randy Bryan. *Thanks Randy.*

My mother and Vanda lived in Waverly, Tennessee, a small town about 70 miles west of Nashville. I moved to a small town called Burns, halfway between Nashville and Waverly. I built a home in a small subdivision and started woodworking as a hobby; my Dad was a carpenter so it came naturally.

Working at Bowne of Nashville

Bowne's office was on the seventeenth floor of the USBank building at Fifth Avenue and Church Street. We covered half of the floor so we could see north, south and west. In the summer of 1998, Randy Bryan walked into the office and informed us a large tornado was heading our way and would arrive in fifteen minutes. We looked out the huge windows and saw it coming from the west. As it hit the Nashville Electric Company, the transformers started exploding — looking like an Independence Day celebration.

I didn't think tornados occurred in Tennessee but it was coming. I was standing about six feet from the windows and saw debris slamming against them; then it got scary, the windows started cracking. We moved farther back, then I felt the floor move. It didn't last long but did extensive damage, yet no one was hurt.

There were three people working in my department at Bowne of Nashville and they were wonderful people with whom to work. They were Sabrina, Bill and Francis.

One slow work day Sabrina and I were looking out the window and chatting when I spotted a building in the distance that looked familiar. I asked her, "What is that building?" She said, "St. Cecilia Academy." I said, "I lived in that building when I was a child and my father was the nuns' chauffeur." She looked surprised. I told her that I also lived in that area when I was a teenager, about 45 years ago. She asked me, "Which Street?" I said, "Ninth Avenue North. I lived across the street from Jones School. I believe the address was 1815 Ninth Avenue North." She jumped out of her chair and screamed — "That is the house I live in." *A small world.*

The next summer a tornado hit my house in Burns. It damaged 200 trees from my three-acre lot. One tree fell on my car and did extensive damage. There was no damage to my house but when I cut all those trees, I had plenty of firewood. I had spent almost thirty years away from Nashville and never had seen a tornado. I returned and in eighteen months, I was in the middle of two. *What are the odds?*

After two years in 1999, Damon moved to Tennessee. I let him stay at my house for a couple of months allowing him to get on his feet. We built our first woodworking project together, a beautiful arbor that still has a place in my yard today.

Damon came to me one day and said, "Dad I played golf today and I loved it." I had tried to get him interested in it when he was younger but he thought golf was for sissies. He took to golf right away and got to be very good. I had not played in 15 years, but I decided to start playing again because of him. We have had many good rounds since that day and I cherish every one. In late 2001 my mom was diagnosed with lung cancer and given one to two years to live.

Time To Hang It Up

I retired from Bowne of Nashville on December 31, 2001. I had worked almost all my adult life but I thought I could find things to keep me busy — golf and wood-working should work. It was a difficult decision but I wanted to take some road trips and enjoy some time off, plus I received a good buy-out. Plus I could have more time with my son.

I have had good jobs that I have chosen, not settled for. I have had many ups and downs, but the ups greatly outnumber the downs.

Sad Times

My mother's lung cancer was getting worse and it was close to the end. I moved her in with me in October 2002 so I could take care of her. She died December 23 of the same year. I lost a great woman that day; my sister Vanda remained with me. I let her stay with me for six months to acclimate her to living without her mother. Which she had lived with for 60 years.

Soon after Mother died Damon and I went on a road trip to East Tennessee to see if he would like the mountains. If so, I wanted to move back to Knoxville but I didn't want to leave him behind. We spent about a week visiting friends and checking out Knoxville and Pigeon Forge and the Smoky Mountains. My plans of moving were dashed when the unexpected happened. (See *next chapter*.)

Paula, Tim, Holly, Allie & Jesse   Dad, Damon, Vanda & Mom

CHAPTER TWELVE

God Made This Decision

T he worst had happened to me. Now the best was coming my way. The next most wonderful woman, Faye Dickens, was coming into my life. I met her in March 2003. After the first date, I went home and told my son, "I'm planning to marry this woman," and showed him a picture of her. She went home and told her friend Pat Perry, I was not for her. *I won that battle.*

I knew I had found the woman for me. I thought she was the finest woman I had ever met. She had beauty inside and outside, and still does.

I enjoyed being with her. Until this day, we have fun just being together.

On our first date she wore over-alls with red pin stripes. Only Faye would do something like that. We met for lunch at O'Charley's Restaurant. She talked the entire time and I listened. I guess because of that she thought I would make a good husband. I knew then I wanted to know more about her.

Faye

91

A few days later I asked her to go on a picnic with me at Montgomery Bell Park. I brought music and drinks and she brought sandwiches. We had a wonderful afternoon and we got to know a little about each other. The music was 50s and 60s, mostly The Platters. I got lucky; she loved the music.

After dating for a couple of months, she wanted me to meet her family especially her three brothers. Wow! Here comes the hard part. I've got to meet the big brothers. Fred lived in California, Bill in North Carolina and Wendell in Tennessee.

They decided to meet in Chattanooga with all the wives, sisters and nieces. I had to please three big brothers to keep dating her. It felt like my teen years — if I didn't please them they might beat me up.

I met them and found out they were super nice people. We had a slumber party and great food. Her sister-in-law was a great cook. We spent the night; the women got to sleep in the beds and the men slept in sleeping bags on the living room floor. The three brothers have since passed away. *Thanks for allowing me to date your sister*.

The people at her church had not seen her with a man in four years so we attracted attention when we entered. The preacher smiled at her from the front of the church and gave her a thumbs-up.

Brother Harold Allen had been knowing Faye for a long time and wanted to meet with me to give me his blessing. He thought God wanted us together. We had lunch at Belle Meade Cafeteria. I guess I got his approval. We asked him to preform the marriage ceremony.

On our next date we went to a movie with some of her friends and went to Krispy Kreme Donut Shop afterwards. One of the friends (Fred) had been watching me for a while and said to her "I noticed he has been touching you often, do you want me to say something to him?" She said, "Don't you dare, I like it."

* * * * *

Faye is smart but sometimes her mouth starts before her brain is in gear. Example:

A well-known street in Nashville is named "Korean Veterans Blvd." As we were driving down this street one day, she saw the street sign and asked, "Why are we honoring their veterans?" *Fayeism*!

* * * * *

After begging her to marry me for a year, she finally said yes. We were married March 20, 2004. Jack Oody kindly came from Knoxville to be my Best Man. *Thank you Jack.*

She messed up my plan to move to Knoxville but I think she's worth the change of plans. This is what lead to our marriage:

Faye and her friends, Burton and Pat Perry had a cruise to the Caribbean planned. The cruise was organized by Burton and Pat's church, so a loaded bus would be traveling from Chattanooga to New Orleans. She asked me if I wanted to go on the cruise with them. I told

93

her I would not go and sleep in separate cabins. I would go if we were married. She said, "Okay we'll get married." So I got a wonderful woman and got my honeymoon paid also. *Boy I'm good.*

* * * * *

After seeing a Pilot Oil tanker (The one with the large coffee cup advertisement on the back of the tank), she said, "Wow that's a lot of coffee." *Fayeism!*

The Honeymoon

The bus trip was an adventure. The driver kept nodding off and I could visualize this huge tour bus running off a mountain and ruining our honeymoon. We were sitting in the seat directly behind him and it was scary. I woke him up twice; then I gave up and went to the back of the bus and located his wife and told her if he didn't wake up, he could kill everyone on the bus. She went to the front and sat with him, talked to him and kept him awake.

We got on board the ship and ate dinner and toured the ship. We had heard about the great midnight buffet but we could not stay up that late.

We were exhausted from the bus trip, so we went to sleep about 9 p.m. I waked and looked at my watch — it was 11:30 p.m. I asked Faye if she wanted to go to the midnight buffet. She always says yes where food is involved, so we dressed and headed to the eating area. We didn't know where it was so I started asking directions. Nobody seemed to know what I was talking about. After asking three people, that looked at me strangely, I found a lady wearing a ship uniform. I asked her, "Where is the midnight buffet?" She looked puzzled and said, "Sir it is 6:30 in the morning." After a little thought, I realized my watch had no numbers, and I had looked at it upside down; it was actually 5:55 a.m. not 11:30 p.m. (*You're gonna check your watch, aren't you?*)

That explained why we didn't see many people on the ship. The ship employee had a story to tell about those dumb Tennesseans. *So we had breakfast.*

The cruise was great and the ship beautiful, food and service were awesome. We had a wonderful time; it was my first cruise but not my last. The honeymoon was also great. The journey was better than the destination.

Faye's Family

Faye is a dedicated Christian and loves going to church. She made me want to be a better person. I felt I had been away from church a long time and promised I would attend with her.

She has a daughter named Paula — a lovely woman. Paula married Tim Jones a week after Faye and I married (Second marriage for both). *Copy cats!*

Tim is a wonderful family man and a good business man. Paula is a businesswoman that has a boutique (Vintage Creek in Whites Creek, Tennessee.) Together they own nine car washes and counting (Champion Car Washes). They love traveling. Unlike Faye and I, they fly to The Caribbean and other exotic places. They don't enjoy the thrill of road trips like Faye and I do.

Paula's son Jesse is a very mature young man of 24 years (Going on 60), gonna be a millionaire (Maybe billionaire) one day. When he was six years old Faye told him we were to be married. He didn't like the idea, so he told Faye, "If you marry Bobby, I'll never come to your house again." After he got to know me, he loved me, and I loved him.

When he was eleven years old, he asked me, "How do you and Nana live without working?" My answer was, "We saved our money and made investments and are living on that money and the dividends it produces." The next day he came to me early in the morning, and asked, "How much money do you need to retire?" An unusual question coming from an eleven-year-old child.

Jesse had a girlfriend when he was about 15 years old, but it didn't work out, so she broke up with him. I asked him if he was okay with the break-up and he said, "I don't mind, she was taking time away from my bush-hogging." Cutting grass was not the foremost thing on my mind when I was 15 years old.

At 21 years old, he bought his first house. He paid 20% down mostly from grass-cutting money. He is making double payments and has opened a ROTH IRA, and has maxed it out for three years as of this writing. His goal is to be a millionaire by age 30. He is now 24 and manages seven car washes for Tim and Paula. He has a wonderful girlfriend named Rebecca (Becca) Anderson, who works for Tim and Paula as their bookkeeper. He loves to mow grass on his off days. I think he will still be cutting grass after he is a millionaire. *I love them all.*

96

Paula and Tim welcomed me into the family with open arms. Both are hard working, successful people. Tim has two beautiful daughters, Allie and Holly Beth. Holly Beth is one of our Super Heroes who works in the ER at Vanderbilt Hospital as a nurse, saving lives. Allie graduated from MTSU. Then she moved to Florida to get her Bachelor of Science at College of Media and Entertainment. She also got her Master's in Education.

Setting Up Housekeeping

Faye lived on a farm in Joelton, Tennessee, where she and her late husband had lived, so that is where we resided. I sold my home in Burns soon after we married and lived on the farm for a year. I really downsized, moving from 4,200 sq. ft. into 1,500 sq. ft. I was okay with it. It made her happy being close to her family. Why would we need that much space?

We have a great doctor, Doctor Fred Nordquist in Pleasant View. The first visit he asked me, "Do you have any hobbies?" I answered, "Yes I play golf." He said, "I've played a few times but I'm not very good." I told him, "Doctor, golf is like sex, you don't have to be good to have fun." He is a wonderful Doctor. He's the reason I'm still alive.

New England Road Trip

We went to Maine as part of our New England trip to see the fall colors. We decided we would stay in Cape Cod for one day. A fun part of that road trip for Faye was the Thrift Stores in Cape Cod. She was like a child in a toy store with everything on sale. She found some wonderful name-brand clothes in those stores: wonderful clothes donated by the rich and famous and sold at low prices. We went from store to store until it was getting late in the day. She wanted to extend the stay one more day because she was getting such great bargains. I told her, "One more day will cost us an extra $100 for a room, three more meals, about $50, and gas to go to all these stores. Would you save enough money on the bargains to make it worthwhile?" She decided to leave; practicality won. That usually doesn't work for us.

On the way back home, we stopped at the Amish country in southern Pennsylvania around Lancaster. We love Amish crafts, and stopped in Intercourse, Bird-In-Hand, Smoketown and Paradise — towns as unique as their names.

We had been looking for a cover for our exposed well pump on the farm and we found something I thought might work. It was a three-foot-square building about five feet tall. It was a replica of an old rustic outhouse and it was on clearance for $40. It was perfect but how would we get it 800 miles back home? It would not fit into the SUV we were driving, but we had bars on top to tie it down. I thought of that image — driving a vehicle with Tennessee tags and carrying our outhouse with us. We finally decided against the idea after a little thought, for safety reasons.

Moving To Springfield

After living on the farm for a year, I wanted a home we could call "our home" so we sold her home and 10 acres of the farm and moved to Springfield, Tennessee. It is a beautiful home and I had room for a 1,300 square foot woodworking shop in the basement.

It was interesting how we found our Springfield home. We saw a builder working on a house in the framing stage and walked through. We loved the floor plan and talked to him about building the same plan for us. We decided we were not ready to move yet.

We started looking for, but not finding, an existing house. We had been looking for a house for some time with no luck. We were close to giving up and building.

As we were driving by the house we saw a year earlier we saw a lady working in the front yard. We stopped and talked to her. Faye told her, "We saw your house being built and love the floor plan." The lady said, "If you will wait a couple of weeks it might be for sale." Wow! I could not believe what I just heard. She explained they could not afford it and were thinking about selling.

We waited and talked about buying it. I told Faye, "Don't get your hopes up; they may not sell. Although we like the floor plan, we don't know if we will like how they painted and trimmed it."

She called two weeks later and said we could look at the house. We hurried to the subdivision and knocked on the door. When we entered we were very surprised: it was as if it had been painted for us. The house was perfect. I told Faye, "We don't have to change anything." The paint, hardwood, and the cabinets, everything was great! We bought the house and moved in a month later.

Hawaiian Cruise

Our Hawaiian cruise was in 2006. It was my favorite cruise ever — our friends Chuck and Jean Pixler joined us and made it a joyous trip. We toured all five islands and rented a Mustang convertible on each island. We spent some time on Waikiki Beach with a view of Diamond Head. *What a gorgeous place!*

Faye collected lava rocks from one of the islands to give to our friends back home. She is always thinking about other people. She put the lava in her purse and carried it with her as we shopped. One shop owner noticed the lava in her purse and said, "You should not take those home with you; it's bad luck." She shrugged her shoulders and we left. We heard from other people that the volcano goddess would be upset if her lava was taken off the island; still she held her ground. When we got to customs to board the ship, the officer told her, "Mrs. Potter, ninety percent of the lava taken off the island is returned within six months, because of people having bad luck." That struck a cord. She pushed the lava to the officer and said, "Take it, take it." *We had extreme good luck when we got back home.*

U.S. Open Golf Tournament

Faye wanted to go to Rockingham, North Carolina to visit her brother Bill McDaniel and his wife Nealie. I was happy to go — it was a road trip. We hit the road and stopped in Knoxville to visit friends. As we left Knoxville on Saturday morning, we noticed the U.S. Open Golf Tournament was being played in Pinehurst,

North Carolina. I grabbed the map to see if Pinehurst was close to Rockingham and it was very close. I asked Faye if she would like to go and of course she said yes.

On the way we saw signs that read: Carolina Auto Parts, Carolina Beauty Shop, Carolina Barber Shop. Faye said, "Carolina must be rich; she owns most of the town." *I love that woman.*

We could make it in time to see the final round on Sunday. I got on the phone and called for tickets. The lady told me the tickets had been sold out for six months. What a letdown, you golfers understand. She also said I might find someone scalping tickets (Illegal to sell tickets over face-value) close to the golf course, but it would be costly. So we took a chance and drove toward the golf course.

We got a couple of miles from the course and I spotted a man sitting in a chair beside his car. I thought, he's a scalper, and pulled over. I asked him if he had tickets to the golf tournament. He said yes, and showed me some tickets. I noticed the price marked on the face was $80. I asked him, "How much for each ticket?" and he said, "$80." I paid him $160 cash and we talked for a while, As we started to leave, he told me he only charged me face-value because he thought I looked familiar and thought I was a cop. He usually charged $200 a ticket. *My lucky day, this ugly mug became an asset.*

I wanted to see Tiger Woods of course, but Jason Gore and Retief Goosen were co-leaders, so we started following them. They made bogey, bogey, bogey on the first three holes, so we went looking for Tiger.

101

We followed him for the remainder of the round. This was one of the greatest thrills of my life! I saw the greatest golfer of all-time play a round of golf and Faye really got caught up in the excitement. She said she loved it, and it was a great experience for her also. Michael Campbell was the eventual winner.

After the tournament, we continued the short trip to Rockingham. After spending a pleasant night with Bill and his wife Nealie, Bill took us to **his** greatest sports arena — the Rockingham Speedway. We toured the track and there was no race that day so we were able to tour all of the facilities with no crowds. One of the drivers took Faye for a few high-speed laps around the track in an official race car — another great experience for my wife.

Damon often babysat our Dachshund, Lady while we were on our trips and one occasion things went bad. His roommate had a Pit Bull that got in an altercation with Lady and Lady was brave but the Pit Bull was too much for her. Lady stayed in the doggie hospital for a few days and they got her back in shape. Damon was devastated by what happened and felt it was his fault and paid for all the vet bills. We assured him it was not his fault, it was life and life happens.

Damon's and Vanda's First Cruise

Faye and I decided to take a cruise with Vanda, Damon and his girlfriend, Jamie. None of them had been on a ship prior. During the cruise, Vanda celebrated her sixty-fourth birthday; the crew gave her a terrific celebration, like she had never seen. They gave her a delicious chocolate cake with chocolate icing. The entire crew of waiters sang Happy Birthday to her. She had never received anything like it.

When we went ashore, she swam in the ocean, sunk a few times, but all in fun. I don't think the smile ever left her face. It was a joyous cruise — I had my wife, my son and my sister with me. *It doesn't get any better*.

Damon loved Jamie and I always hoped they would get married, but things didn't work out that way. They quit seeing each other later. *I suppose he is like his Dad; women get tired of him quickly.*

Another New England Trip

Our next trip to New England was wonderful. We took our time and didn't plan anything, like most of our road trips. We had a book outlining the best things to see in New England, so we followed some of them. One of its recommendations was Red's Eats, known for having the best lobster rolls in Maine. We traveled over one hundred miles out of our way to get a lobster roll. *It was worth it.*

We arrived and there was a long line. It was a tiny place, a building about 12' by 12'. It didn't look like the kind of place that sells "The best lobster rolls in Maine," as it was advertised. There were about fifteen people in front of us when we started waiting. As we stood there, the line kept getting longer. When we finally got to the front of the line, we ordered through a small window in the front of the building and we asked for two lobster rolls. When the order arrived, they were lobster served on an open hoagie bun. The lady said, "$40 dollars please." My wife said, in her loud Tennessee voice, "Forty dollars for two hotdogs?" That is what I love about her, straight to the point. We ate the rolls at a picnic table behind the building. The lobster rolls were delicious, as advertised.

Most people would not drive a hundred miles for lobster rolls, but I believe it's not about the destination; it's about the journey.

We arrived in Bar Harbor to stay a few days and checked into a motel and got a room on the second floor. We carried a couple of suitcases to the room. Faye went out on the balcony to admire the view and I opened the suitcases and hung some clothes in the closet. I went back down to get the rest of our luggage and saw two women coming up. I overheard them in the middle of a conversation. One said, "Why was she waving at you?" The other one said, "I don't know, I was sitting in my car and she was looking at me and waving her arm and smiling." (These women obviously didn't know about the Tennessee tradition of friendly waving.) I said, "I think that would be my wife." I just left them looking puzzled. When I got back to the room, I asked Faye if she had been waving at a woman. She said, "Yes, but she didn't wave back." *I love Bar Harbor.*

The next morning we headed to Cadillac Mountain to watch the sunrise. As we joined about fifty other sightseers, the sun was barely peeking over the horizon. About that time, we saw a dozen women clad in long white robes; everyone was staring at them, including us. After about ten minutes, a brave lady asked them if they belonged to a cult, and one answered, "No, it was cold and we didn't have coats, so we borrowed these robes from the motel."

Lake Champlain

As we were in New England, my ex-wife begged to help with our schedule. We don't like to have a schedule but she was so nice to book it we agreed. She booked us a stay at Lake Champlain.

We were running behind on our schedule and was in Maine and had to be two states away the next day. We left Maine early Thursday morning and arrived at Lake Champlain in two days.

We arrived early Friday night in time to get our room. It was dark so we could not see well. The place was in the middle of nowhere, antiquated single-story row of rooms. We were the only people to be seen. I started thinking, "Bates Motel."

We went to the office and met a nice, attractive and friendly young lady at the desk. She told us breakfast was served in the dining room the following morning. We paid for three nights.

We walked into the room and was surprised. The place was neat and clean but sparsely furnished. Something was strange about this room. There was no television, no phone and no coffee maker. This place had the bare necessities.

My first thought was: we have been had. We were tired and as we went to bed we heard a car drive in and heard voices. We knew then we were not alone so we felt better and went to sleep.

We awoke the next morning, walked outside and was shocked. The parking lot was full of cars and the surroundings were beautiful in the light. We headed to the dining room and were greeted by a gracious gentleman who introduced himself as the waiter and cook. He was also married to the lady who greeted us the night before.

We sat down and he brought us one of the best meals we had ever eaten. Wonderful wild blueberry pancakes, that were the best.

We figured out what was going on. Busy people from New York City wanted a get-away at the end of a hectic week. They didn't want to see television or use a phone. They wanted peace and quiet. This was perfect.

We spent three wonderful days at that beautiful place. I have thanked my ex-wife many times for the help.

We learned the man and wife ran the motel in the summer and ran a ski lodge in the winter.

Caribbean Cruise

Another cruise was in 2010. This cruise was to the southern Caribbean. We were on the way to our ship for the cruise and were driving south on Highway 41 on the eastern side of Florida. We were a little hungry so we began looking for a place to eat. We were approaching a small town called Masaryktown, one of those little one-horse towns. We stopped for gas at the only gas station in town, filled up and asked directions to an eating place.

A man said the only place in town was a little cafe down the road called Cafe Masaryktown, and they had good Cuban sandwiches. We pulled into the little quaint restaurant and it looked okay, so we entered and took a seat. The waitress came to our table and I asked her what she recommended. She said, "The Cuban sandwiches are very good," so we ordered Cuban sandwiches. After a short wait, she returned with two delicious sandwiches. We were surprised we got something that good in a little town called Masaryktown.

We continued our trip to Fort Lauderdale and boarded our cruise ship. It was around five p.m., so we were getting hungry and headed for the dining area. We each got a plate and found a table. An older couple came and sat at the table closest to us. As usual Faye struck up a conversation with them. They told us they were on their honeymoon and they seemed to be a very happy couple. My wife asked them where they were from, and her answer was, "A little town you never heard of called Masaryktown, Florida." So we told them about Cafe Masaryktown and the Cuban sandwiches we had for lunch, and she said she lives across the street from Cafe Masaryktown. *Small world, huh?*

Interesting People

The next day we entered the crowded dining hall and selected our lunch from the buffet. As we were walking around looking for a vacant table, an older man who looked like he had lived a rough life, sitting at a table for four, motioned for us to sit down. We joined him and thanked him for his courtesy. He looked to be about 90-

107

plus years old. He was dressed in very nice casual clothes. He had a soft voice, the kind you could listen to for hours. I asked him his name and where he was from, and he said he was from Chicago and his name was Gus. I asked him what kind of work he did — that was all it took for this interesting man to tell us his story. We just sat and listened.

He said he had been a truck driver from his teens until he retired a few years earlier. He said he had driven trucks for a lot of people including Al Capone — that perked my ears up. He said he delivered booze and slot machines for Capone and his competition, which was bootlegged in the days of prohibition.

We sat with Gus quietly and listened to every word this interesting man was relating to us.

He had driven for anyone who would give him a job. He would never join the Teamsters Union because he didn't want anyone telling him how to do his job. He had many attempts on his life and one of them happened one night as he was driving along on a lonely highway, and a long black car pulled alongside of him. The passenger held up a 45-caliber automatic pistol, where he could see he meant business, and shouted for him to pull over. He said he kept on driving and they ran him off the road. He wrecked his truck but he was unharmed and they continued on down the highway.

Gus said he had driven the mob guys out in the wilderness to do their evil deeds to someone with whom they had displeasure. He would wait in the truck and usually the victim didn't come back.

Another time, the bad guys instructed him to take a man for a ride. When they got to the destination, they asked Gus to get out of the truck and come with them. They told him to kneel with the other guy, in front of them. They then put a gun to the guy's temple and shot him, they then told Gus to get in the truck and drive them back. *Scary stuff.*

Another story Gus told us: he was hired to deliver a load of slots for Capone and was pulled over by Capone's competition. They got out with guns drawn and opened the back of his truck and found it empty; he was a decoy! The slots were in another truck. I was unnerved just listening to Gus tell us this story. How scared he must have been.

I have never seen my wife sit so long and not say a word; she was engrossed in Gus' stories.

He told us some other stories that day which I don't remember. Everybody has stories — some true, some not so true. I believed that gentleman; he looked the part and knew all the details.

We did not see Gus for the remainder of our cruise. *Thank you Gus, for those intriguing stories.*

For dinner we were assigned a table for four so another couple joined us. They were a nice couple from Northern California — Suze and Dick Trost. We had a lot in common with them.

We liked them so much we spent almost the entire cruise hanging out with them. We went to shows together at night and we spent a lot of time ashore with them also.

After the fourth night of dinner with them, for the first time, we headed to our cabins together. We walked to the other end of the ship, got on the elevator and got off at the same level. I started to wonder where they were going. There were four levels on this ship and it was very long, and they were still with us. Why were they going the same way as we were? We walked down the narrow corridor for a long way. Faye and I stopped and said, "This is our cabin." Suzy said, "This is ours across from you." Of the hundreds of people on board, we ate together, hung out together and lived directly across from each other. *What are the odds?*

We stopped in beautiful Maggie Valley, North Carolina and stayed at a motel on the way home. This place is one of the most beautiful places on earth. The next morning we walked out on the balcony and saw about 50 Chevy SSRs (Chevrolet Sport truck, body style of a 1940s truck but with modern technology) in the parking lot — a rainbow of colors. I didn't know there were that many in the world. We found out later it was a meeting of SSR owners. I love old cars, but I don't like the maintenance I would have to do to keep one up to date, so I've never bought one.

Quest For An SSR

I still had those cars on my mind when we came back home. Then fate happened — two of our friends came to our house for a visit and pulled into the driveway in a beautiful blue SSR. The first words out of my mouth were, "I want one of those."

110

They were made for only four years, from 2003 through 2006. The years 2005 and 2006 were the best because those had Corvette engines. I started looking for one and decided I wanted red or black. I looked for two months and found one in Greenville, South Carolina. I called the guy and we worked out a deal. The next day Faye and I flew to Charlotte, North Carolina and rented a car and drove to Greenville, South Carolina. The owners were Bill and Tina Barnes, super nice people, and they invited us to dinner and fed us a great meal. They also asked us to spend the night, which we graciously refused because we already had a motel room. *Bill and Tina know how to sell a car.*

Their son didn't like the idea of us eating with them or the fact we were invited to spend the night — good son looking out for his parents' well being.

The car was beautiful. It was a 2005 red beauty with black upholstery and was parked in the garage on a large piece of carpet. The car had no dirt anywhere, not even underneath. The car had never been driven in the rain; it had a racing chip built-in to increase the horsepower from 390 HP to 530 HP. I don't remember the exact mileage but it was very low.

We made the deal and headed home, and of course something bad had to happen. It started raining and rained all the way home; I called Bill and told him I was sorry but his car was getting its initial rain. Bill died shortly after we returned home with the SSR. *Sorry for such a short life buddy. RIP*

111

More Road Trips

H&H Restaurant in Macon, Georgia, came into my life again forty years later. Faye and I were in Augusta, Georgia and I told her about the restaurant in Macon where Scottie and I had eaten years before and she said, "Let's go find it." I didn't remember the name or location, but we looked up restaurants online in Macon, and the name H&H looked familiar. We found it, much to my surprise! While we were ordering, I talked to the manager, who was one of the original owner's granddaughter, I told her my story; it made her happy I had known her Grandmother. *Wonderful soul food.*

Back In Springfield

Faye and Vanda went to Montgomery Bell Golf Course to practice hitting golf balls with me and I got them a bucket of balls. After hitting a few balls I returned to my car to get more tees and when I was walking back to the practice tee I didn't see Faye and Vanda. The practice tee box is elevated so I could not see the entire landing area. When I got closer I saw them out on the range picking up balls and filling up their buckets. I told them they were not supposed to be on the range. They needed to go to the club house and pay for more balls. Faye's answer was, "I don't know why we can't use these, nobody is using them." *Sounded good to me.*

Vanda Moving

Years ago, I had asked Dad to let Vanda live alone and get her a tutor, so she could live a normal life, but he refused. She always wanted to live alone, so Faye and I got her an apartment about a five-minute drive from where we lived. We took her shopping and took care of her needs; she was happy living by herself and her little dog.

Faye accepted Vanda as part of the family. She helped me take care of her groceries, utilities and shopping. We visited her at least once a week and included her in most of our activities including eating out. She could not manage money, so we did that for her.

Mom and Dad never legally declared Vanda incompetent so I could not control where she lived. We tried to influence her and get the best for her, but I had no legal control over her.

After she had stayed in her apartment for about two years, she wanted to move to Erin, Tennessee (A small town about 60 miles from me). She had a cousin that could take care of her money. I had promised my mother I would take care of her and I needed her close to achieve that. I was not in favor of her moving.

One day Faye and I went to visit her and she had moved out. She knew we would not like her moving so she sneaked out at night. We had no control so we had to let her go. She has managed her life since that time without me, not without hiccups but she has survived, which mades me proud of her.

Moving Again

After seven years of living in Springfield, Faye felt we needed to move because the house was too large for two people. We could not find a house we liked, so we decided to build. The only appealing lot we found was in

Greenbrier. Remember, my mother's birth town was Greenbrier, Tennessee.

This is a weird circumstance about Greenbrier. When I was young, Mom and Dad would make me go to Greenbrier to visit her relatives. I always thought Greenbrier was a hick town and boring, so I vowed that when I grew up, I would never set foot in Greenbrier again. Faye and I bought the lot and built our home. After traveling all over the United States and Canada, visiting 49 states, and I returned and we moved to Greenbrier. I had just gone full circle. I love Greenbrier. It's so quiet and peaceful. It is still a hick town but I love hick towns.

We built a beautiful 2,200 square foot home. We wanted it to look old, like it was built in the early 1900s. We gave it a Craftsman Style, inside and outside. We have pegs on the wall for hanging chairs and clothing like our ancestors did. We painted the walls pale colors and the trim medium brown. We furnished it with primitive furniture and accessories. Faye has a six-foot-tall colorful metal rooster in the front yard. Some of our friends ask why we don't buy new furniture: We say, "We have the furniture we want." *We are the talk of the neighborhood; some of the talk might be positive.*

We have friends we meet for dinner about once a week: Mike and Mary Carty, Bob and Judy Brewer, Norman and Jeanette Marshall. Also Bob and Carolyn Morgan until Bob died last year. Carolyn still joins us.

One day we reserved a table for seven at Liz's Restaurant in Goodlettsville for lunch after church. I was the first to arrive at the busy restaurant and saw a long line outside. I entered and informed the waitress I had a reservation for four but didn't see our table. She said she knew nothing about the reservation. She pointed to a table for four and said, "You can have that table and ask the elderly lady setting by herself at a table for four and push the tables together." I asked the lady, "Would you like to have a party." She said she would and I joined her and waited for my friends.

As I was ordering I felt sorry for the lady dining by herself and was nice to let us join her so I told the waitress to give me her check. The waitress later brought me and my wife's checks along with the lady's. I slid it under the salt shaker without looking and continued talking to my friends.

When our new lady friend finished her meal she headed for the cashier. Then she headed back to our table with her arms full of to-go boxes and said, "I want to thank you for lunch, and my husband and son and daughter . . . thank you." I lost her at daughter; I didn't know I was feeding an entire family but I told her I wanted to thank her for letting us join her.

* * * * *

We have continued the road trips: three-week trips to New England three times, four-week trip to the western states, one-week trip to Texas, one-week trip to Florida, a few trips to North Carolina to visit Faye's brother, and many trips to Gatlinburg, Tennessee. The difference now is we have a place to call home.

Damon & Bobby

Damon, Warren & Henry

Bobby & Faye

Jesse & Becca

Bobby & Damon

Trine & Damon

Damon

Faye

Bobby, Damon & Scottie

Damon & Scottie

Jamie & Damon

Damon & Donna

118

CHAPTER THIRTEEN

Damon Martin Potter

D amon has always been Faye's guinea pig. She liked to try new recipes on him. The agreement was: she would try a new recipe. If Damon didn't like a meal, she would not make it again. Most of the time she made great dishes, but one day she screwed up the pot roast; it tasted pretty badly. Damon ate it without saying a word. Afterwards he told her, "Faye, you don't have to make this one again." *Always the gentleman.*

Damon and I met for breakfast at Noshville Restaurant one morning before he went to work and got caught up on things. After arriving home, Faye asked me where we had eaten and I told her Noshville Restaurant. She said, "Oh, the one on 21st Avenue?" I informed her it was on Broadway. She didn't believe me, and kept repeating, "It is on 21st." I said, "Honey, I just left there, I know which street it is on." She called the restaurant and asked them their address. The lady said, "1905 Broadway." Faye paused and said, "When did you move?" The lady told her they had never moved. Pretty stubborn, right? *You gotta love her.*

Damon has been in sales for most of his adult life, and he worked for Jim Reed Chevrolet as a Finance Manager. He visited Faye and I almost every Sunday. We would watch football or golf on TV, and he would help me with my chores — the things I couldn't handle, like climbing ladders. I'm afraid of heights. He also helped me built

119

many projects in my Woodshop. If he had any weekdays off, we would play golf. We had a lot of fun and our games were equal. Faye treated him as her child, and he loved her like a mother.

Damon called me one day and informed me he was going to Kentucky to help a friend take care of his wife. She had suffered through a difficult childbirth. He stayed with them for two weeks which were weeks he lost work. He was always willing to help his friends.

One year he told me he had a friend in Florida who organized a football pool he had entered. Everyone put in $20 and picked winners each week on NFL games. The season had already started so I could not join. There was $6,000 in the pot. He had no experience in picking ball games so I helped him. Each week I gave him two to three games and let him pick one. Lucky kid won every week and won the pot.

He and I often worked in my woodworking shop and built stuff out of wood. We built many outdoor furniture pieces, and I loved the quality time we shared together.

He had an anger problem. He was able to control it by wearing a rubber band on his wrist, stretching it and letting it go — snapping against his skin. The sharp pain would remind him to pause and think.

I called him one day and he seemed to have something bothering him and I asked him if he had a problem with me. He told me he was upset because I didn't spend more time with him when he was younger. I asked him to come and visit and we could talk it over.

He arrived the next day and we went into the den and had a serious conversation. He said, "Dad you didn't spend time with me when I was younger and you didn't come see my tennis matches." I told him, "You are right, I didn't spend enough time with you. I wish I could go back and make it right."

"I gave up gambling because I didn't want you exposed to that kind of life. In return I had to take the managing job and work 12 hours a day to pay our expenses: like house payment, car payments, college tuition and food. I worked all those years trying to put away enough money for you to be comfortable when I died. I believed I made the right decision at that time. If I could go back and make that decision again, I would probably have a better balance. If you think I was wrong, I apologize, and want you to know I made that decision because I loved you very much."

He seemed to understand and gave me a hug. That was the only big misunderstanding we had in our life.

He moved to Florida a few years later, in 2015, for a job offer at a car dealership. The job didn't pan out, so he ran out of money after a month. *Sounds like his Dad.*

He was living in his car; then something great happened. He met a woman named Trine Andersen and fell in love; she learned of his situation and asked him to move in with her. They lived together happily for four years. *Thank you Trine, for taking care of my little boy.*

He came to visit Faye and I about twice a year. It was always wonderful to see him. He came to visit us in the middle of May 2019, and we played golf at Legacy Golf Club. As we were on the first tee, an older gentleman joined us and while we were playing, he told us a story about his father dying and how he regretted not seeing more of him. Damon looked sad and told me, "Dad, you are going to see more of me from now on."

He came back to visit on Friday, May 31, to celebrated our birthdays: his on May 31 and mine on June 2. He arrived and stayed with friends, promising us he would meet us the next day for lunch. Faye was a little under the weather Saturday, so we called it off; he was leaving the next day, but said he would be back soon.

Extreme Devastation

The next morning I texted him a few times, but didn't get a reply. We decided to go to plan B and we asked some friends, Bill and Patricia Standley, to have a birthday lunch with us at Red Lobster. Patricia agreed but Bill didn't feel well so he declined.

We were in the middle of lunch and Faye got a call from Trine. She told us something that made me feel like my chest was going to explode: **"Damon is dead."**

At the young age of 43, a perfectly healthy man went to sleep and didn't wake up. Even to this day, two years later, tears are running down my cheeks as I write this.

After hearing the news, Patricia told us to go see Damon and she would take care of the check. We must have attracted attention; after we left a man approached Patricia and inquired about what was happening. She told him my son had died and he said, "Give me the check."

He paid for our meal and told Patricia how sorry he was. There are a lot of wonderful people in this world. I don't know who he was, *but thank you sir, you're a very kind person*. I will return your kindness to someone needing a lift in the future.

Faye and I rushed to Summit Hospital, hoping the news was wrong and I would see my son alive. After arriving, we talked to a doctor and got confirmation, he had died at 11 a.m. on June 2, 2019. He was so surprised that a healthy young male, with no signs of trauma, would die. I looked at his lifeless body laying on that cold slab, and thought, "Damon, I am so sorry I could not protect you from this." Later it was confirmed he had died of a heart attack.

Damon was a health nut and was diligent about taking care of his body. He ate well and went to the gym regularly. One would think that would be enough to keep him alive until he reached an older age.

He only lived half of his life. I have been trying to keep my mind and body busy to cope with this agony. **Not only I lost my child, but also my child losing the promise of a future life.** Damon was cremated and his mother took his ashes back to Houston with her. He is back in Texas where he was born.

The sad things I've had in my life were just speed bumps compared to what I have felt since June 2, 2019. Damon was such a kind man. I have to keep reminding myself to keep-on, keeping-on. When the world tells me to give up; I try harder.

123

Traveling Looks Different Now

Although I think Tennessee is the most beautiful place I've ever been, except maybe Hawaii, I still have urges to throw a suitcase into the car and hit the road again.

I have some ailments that slow me down but I do most of the things I once did. I have Diabetes, Asthma, Bladder cancer, Neuropathy, Arthritis, and Fibromyalgia. I have a few stumbling blocks but they don't stop me, I have determination!

My body may feel 81 years old but my mind works as if I am 40 years old. I can no longer manage those long road trips but we occasionally take one or two-day trips. I play golf when the weather permits. Last summer I shot lower than my age (79). That was a great thrill.

We have been living in this house for over eight years. I never lived in one place that long. Am I settling down? Nah, I'll be on the road to Alaska any day.

* * * * *

I want to thank my golfing partners for putting up with my shenanigans all these years. They are Bill Putman and Brent Poulton. If you will notice, all of our initials are BP. I usually keep score and I put our initials on the scorecard. When I add the score, the lowest score is mine. *Clever, huh?*

Also, thanks to David Alexander, who played with us, but as of this writing is very sick. *Get well soon David.*

Joe Batson was a playing partner for years and has passed. *Rest in peace Joe.*

* * * * *

This book has been stressful but I felt I needed to write it. It will be something I can leave behind for friends and Faye's family. It was difficult to write about the friends and family I have lost over the years. My family will end with my death. Damon was my only child and my sister did not have children.

People tell me the grief gets easier. I don't know if it does. The only thing that is better is: I break down less often as I once did. It still hurts just as badly. **Damon died once but I die everyday**.

It hurts but I believe if I keep my mind and body busy I'll be able to handle it.

I carry a few five and ten dollar bills with me. When I see a young child I think I could make happy, I give them one. It makes me happy to share a little of the things I have received in my lifetime. Life has been good to me. I enjoy giving some back.

I have discovered what is around the next curve and what is at the end of the road. It is what you make it!

Memorial to Damon

I erected a three-foot-high cross just outside my den window under a beautiful pink Dogwood tree. On the cross I burned a message that reads:

Your Life Was A Blessing
Your Memory Is A Treasure
You Are Loved Beyond Words
Missed Beyond Measure

Damon's Cross & Dogwood Tree

126

ACKNOWLEDGEMENT

I am not famous, nor am I wealthy. I am just a normal American male that has been knocked down many times in life, but always gotten back up and tried again.

I believe I am a better person than I have ever been. I owe the happiness I feel to my wife Faye. I have come a long way; it has not all been easy, but it has all been worthwhile.

I am writing this book for my family and the people that care about me or anyone just curious to know about my life. I am writing by memory, so if I have made a mistake about dates or names, please forgive me. I am 81 years old and memory is not my forte.

Everything in this book actually happened. Some of it I'm ashamed of and some of it I'm proud of, but I learned from it and believe I learn something new every day of my life.

I am not recommending or condoning anything in this book. I'm just telling what I did in my life, everyone should determine right from wrong and act on that knowledge. Some of the things I did turned out right, some turned out wrong. I think as a person the end result turned out fair.

Some of the things in this book I have lived with all my life and never told anyone.

If this book helps or entertains one person, it will be worth the effort.

**If there is a message in my story, it is:
Don't ever give up.**

**We all have made choices that perhaps weren't
the best ones. None of us are completely innocent, but we all get a fresh start every day to
be a better person than we were yesterday.**

**I want to thank everyone that helped me
with this book, Brent Poulton for writing the
Foreword, John Bumgardner for his advise,
Terri Morris for the beautiful cover and
Scottie for her proofreading and
jogging my memory.**

**Thanks to my wife Faye for her patience
and encouragement.**

WHY I WROTE THIS BOOK

I wanted to do something for my son that would create a lasting memory of him for family and friends.

I thought about leaving a charity donation and create a plaque with his name, date of birth and death but he was not famous so nobody would know the person he was.

So I decided to write this book. It is not a literary masterpiece, maybe not even enjoyable reading but I hope I told enough of his life that people will know the good things about him.

He was a very private person and didn't like to talk about himself so I didn't know his inner thoughts. But he was a wonderful human being and I told all I remember about him.

I know writing this book has done me good. I have spent two miserable years since his death blaming myself and God for what happened to him. When I finished this book I felt like I had a great weight lifted from me and I felt a wonderful peace.

9 780578 916781